A Word from the Author of
CORRECT SPELLING MADE EASY

"I promise you this: when you have finished your training in Chapter 49, you will not only be unable to spell a word incorrectly, but you will be supremely self-confident— and have every justification for such confidence—that nothing you ever write is ever marred by spelling errors."

A WORD ABOUT THE AUTHOR OF CORRECT SPELLING MADE EASY: Norman Lewis, author and teacher, is famous for his adult education courses at New York University and City College. He has written many volumes on spelling, pronunciation, and grammar, including the highly successful BETTER ENGLISH, the book that takes the pedantry out of correct English.

ALSO AVAILABLE IN LAUREL:

BETTER ENGLISH
by Norman Lewis

Fail to do what is wanted or
expected

(D-) .... (DISAPPOINT)

State incorrectly

(M-) .... (MISSTATE)

False step

(M-) .... (MISSTEP)

Give a bad or ugly shape to

(M-) .... (MISSHAPE)

State of being self-conscious,
ill at ease, uncomfortable

(E-) .... (EMBARRASSMENT)

Process of enveloping

(E-) .... (ENVELOPMENT)

Paraphernalia; necessary tools,
furniture, machinery, etc.

(E-) .... (EQUIPMENT)

Chapter 4.
-IE AND -EI

Which combination do you think is commoner in English spelling, -IE or -EI? Reflect on this question for a moment, and you're likely to make the proper choice . . . -IE. Words like *field, relieve, niece, shriek, priest, brief,* and scores of others readily spring to mind.

So when do we use -EI? Examine the following carefully, rewriting each one:

RECEIVE ....

RECEIPT ....

CONCEIVE ....

CONCEIT ....

DECEIVE ....

DECEIT ....

PERCEIVE ....

CEILING ....

Discovering a Rule

The eight examples you have just examined have the same long E sound heard in -IE words like *field, relieve, niece,* etc. How come, then, -EI? What is the common, and special, element in these eight odd-balls? Look at them again —and put your answer, which should be extremely brief, on the following line:

i comes before e except after c and doesn't have a sh sound.

CORRECT SPELLING MADE EASY

BY NORMAN LEWIS

A LAUREL ORIGINAL

PUBLISHED BY DELL PUBLISHING CO., INC.
1 Dag Hammarskjold Plaza, New York, N.Y. 10017

Laurel ® TM 674623, Dell Publishing Co., Inc.

ISBN: 0-440-31502-6

DEDICATION: For Mary, Margie and Debbie

ACKNOWLEDGMENT: I particularly wish to acknowledge
a debt to my secretary, Scottie Walters, whose
remarkable efficiency and cheerful presence made
this work move along more smoothly
than I had thought possible.

First printing—May, 1963
Second printing—March, 1965
Third printing—November, 1965
Fourth printing—March, 1967
Fifth printing—September, 1968
Sixth printing—October, 1969
Seventh printing—November, 1970
Eighth printing—September, 1971
Ninth printing—August, 1972
Tenth printing—February, 1974
Eleventh printing—September, 1974
Twelfth printing—April, 1975
Thirteenth printing—April, 1976
Fourteenth printing—February, 1977
Fifteenth printing—April, 1978

Contents

Chapter 1.

HOW TO USE THIS BOOK TO BECOME
AN EXPERT IN SPELLING

Everyone Makes Mistakes

The chances are very good that some letter, report, theme, business memo, or other communication you write within the next week will contain one or more errors in spelling.

The chances are even better that you will be unaware that you've misspelled any words, though, ironically, your mistake (or mistakes) will be glaringly conspicuous to your reader, who thereupon, charitably inclined though he may otherwise be, will immediately have a lower opinion of your ability or worth than he had before.

As I say, this is ironic, for your reader very likely has his own troubles; but in spelling as in so many other areas of life, we can easily spot the mote in the other fellow's eye while being completely unaware of the beam in our own.

For it is a fact that few people, no matter how literate or well-educated, ever attain real expertness in English spelling without careful training. What's more, it is the rare person, indeed, who possesses absolute self-assurance about his ability to spell correctly, or who has any security that he can write a completely error-free paper.

Everyone makes mistakes, and generally in the most common and frequently used words; and each person has a pet list of one hundred or so special demons that he always gets wrong.

This pet list may vary considerably from person to person, as I have indicated, but *almost every word on everybody's list is sure to be among the 1,100 words covered in this book*—1,100 words that are particularly prone to misspelling. These words, more than any others in the whole language, cause all the grief, all the confusion, and all the frustration that afflict writers who have never been thoroughly and methodically trained in the complexities and inconsistencies of the system of spelling under which we operate.

This book offers you precisely the thorough and methodical training that will make you an expert, self-assured speller in a surprisingly short time.

How This Book Is Organized

Correct Spelling Made Easy is composed of 50 chapters so designed that you can successfully cover each one in a single sitting. The chapters are of different length—some, comparatively short, train you to conquer 10 to 15 demons, and will take no more than a quarter hour of your time; others, somewhat longer, will make you master of up to 35 or 40 words, and may require three quarters of an hour of study; a few are review or test chapters aimed at making permanent the learning of five or more previous days, and can be covered in a few minutes. *At most, then, working only 15-45 minutes a day, you can, if you are willing to apply yourself, become an expert speller in under two months.*

Applying yourself will be easy—and not only easy, which is little enough to say for your experience with a book such as this, but, more important, stimulating, exciting, and challenging every step of the way. And most important of all, *rewarding*—for each day you will sense new power and self-confidence as you conquer, once and for all, the words that almost everyone else misspells or is confused by.

How You Train Yourself to Become an Expert Speller

The minute you start the next chapter you will understand why your training has to be successful, no matter how incorrigibly poor a speller you may consider yourself today.

For, to begin with, you do not passively *read* this book—you actively *work* in it, page by page, pencil always in

<u>hand.</u> (Don't optimistically provide yourself with a pen—every so often you may have to erase and try again.)

As soon as you make your <u>first contact with a word in its correct form, your eyes will be directed to that area where the error always creeps in</u>. Every word in our list of 1,100 has such an area, underlined boldly by a black line. (A very few of the words may have two, or, occasionally, three areas of error, but those are rare.) You will thus immediately learn where your mistake is likely to occur, and what to do about it. This, then, will be the first step in training your *visual memory*.

Next, you will be asked to conceal the word with an index or playing card, a piece of blank paper, or your hand—and <u>immediately rewrite it</u>. (This is the first step in training your *<u>muscular memory</u>*—in developing in your fingers a kind of automatic accuracy.) Then you uncover the word and check your response. If you're right, your learning will be reinforced; if error persists, you erase and make another attempt. Constantly, throughout the book, you are driving deeper and deeper, almost into the unconscious levels of your mind, the correct patterns of words, obliterating what may have formerly been your incorrect responses, until finally proper spellings become unhesitating, reflexive, automatic; misspellings become virtually impossible.

You will go through this process several times with each word in a chapter, both in the body of the material and in the practice exercises—and still once again, after a time lapse, when the word is repeated in the review chapters.

(<u>Please remember, whenever you test yourself in the practice exercises and in the review chapters, to check your responses *immediately*</u>, in order, as I have said, to *<u>reinforce</u>* correct learning and *obliterate* all memory of unsuitable reactions.)

As you will shortly notice, every response demanded of you will occur in a meaningful situation. <u>You will have to *think* as you write—there will never be any danger of your being distracted or getting lost in wool-gathering, for then no real learning takes place.</u>

And I promise you this: when you have finished your training in chapter 49, you will not only be unable to spell a word incorrectly, but you will be supremely self-confident (and have every justification for such confidence) that nothing you ever write is marred by spelling errors.

The Kind of Words You Will Study

What sort of words do educated people misspell?

Words that could just as logically have a double consonant where a single one is correct—or, of course, vice versa.

Words in which an unaccented syllable looks good with one vowel, but another is right.

Words that end in -ABLE or -IBLE; -ANCE or -ENCE; -ANT or -ENT; -ARY or -ERY; -OR or -ER; -ISE or -IZE.

Words that have an S where one normally expects a C (or vice versa); that have -EI where -IE seems to make sense (or again, vice versa); that retain E where one is irresistibly tempted to drop it, or, contrarily, drop E where logic dictates keeping it in.

In short, words that have two patterns—the correct one, and the one most mediocre spellers are attached to.

And these, for the most part, are common, everyday words used over and over again in a busy week's writing.

Words like DRUNKENNESS from which a poor speller will omit one of the double N's; COOLLY, which he writes with one L; EMBARRASS which he spells with either one R or one S; VACILLATE, in which he uses one L; OCCURRENCE, in which he fails to double the R or substitutes A for E in the ending; INOCULATE, in which he overgenerously doubles the N or the C, or both. And almost 1,100 more, each containing one area which inevitably traps the nonexpert.

A few uncommon or bookish words—like PICCALILLI, TOCCATA, APOCRYPHAL, FRICASSEE, TITILLATE, DILETTANTE, DESICCATE, ESOPHAGUS—are included, though these admittedly do not occur very often in writing. However, when they do occur they are invariably misspelled, or the writer has feverishly thumbed through the dictionary before daring to put them down. (And since he has never learned how to discover the crucial areas of words and store up the proper patterns in his visual memory, he will go scurrying to the dictionary every time he has occasion to use them.)

Spelling Rules

Rules are not neglected in the book. Neither are they fussed over, however, and never are you asked to memorize them. (Many poor spellers can quote rules verbatim, but still misspell the words that the rules cover.) Instead, you tackle the words first, then realize that rules are arbitrarily devised to explain similarity of patterns. In this way you really understand each rule and can automatically apply it without cluttering your memory with a lot of abstract principles.

Why This Book Is Guaranteed to Make You a Better Speller

Whether you consider yourself a fairly good, a mediocre, or even a hopelessly poor speller, within two months, if you work hard and follow all instructions carefully, you *must* improve. And not only improve, but become skillful far beyond the average, indeed come close to infallibility.

For whatever words you unconsciously write incorrectly, whatever words puzzle or stump you, are in this list of 1,100 demons.

These are the words that high school students, college students, college graduates, business people, typists, secretaries, letter writers of all ages and degrees of education, misspell—these and very few, if any, others. And these are the words that you will train your mind to remember correctly, your fingers to spell correctly.

When you have turned the last page of this book, it will be a very rare word indeed that you cannot unhesitatingly spell as easily, and as perfectly, as you spell your own name.

Chapter 2.

VERBS IN -ISE

<u>More verbs end in -IZE than in -ISE.</u>

There are, indeed, hundreds upon hundreds of -IZE verbs, and it's doubtful that you have trouble with any of them.

There's *agonize* and *authorize, baptize* and *brutalize, civilize* and *colonize, disorganize* and *dramatize,* and so on right through the alphabet, ending with *utilize, verbalize, victimize, vocalize,* and *vulcanize,* to say nothing of the little-used *wantonize.*

All -IZE. So it is no wonder that the few handfuls of -ISE verbs get short shrift from casual spellers or cause confusion to conscientious ones.

<u>Of the few -ISE verbs there are, ten especially are commonly misspelled</u>—the ten you will find below.

Start your practice by making a strong visual adjustment to them—get such a clear mental picture of each one with -ISE in the last syllable that no other ending will ever look right to you.

Then cover each word with your card and write it on the blank line to its right. Check at once. Was your mental photograph accurate in every detail?

1. ADVERT<u>ISE</u>   ....
2. CHAST<u>ISE</u>   ....
3. DESP<u>ISE</u>   ....
4. EXERC<u>ISE</u>   ....
5. SURPR<u>ISE</u>   ....

6. ADV<u>ISE</u> ....

7. DEV<u>ISE</u> ....

8. IMPROV<u>ISE</u> ....

9. REV<u>ISE</u> ....

10. SUPERV<u>ISE</u> ....

More Practice

If I start you off with the first few letters of each word, can you successfully finish it in the -ING form? (That is, *chastising*, etc.). Note that the final E will of course be dropped before -ING. Write the complete word in the blank, not just the remaining letters. Keep each answer covered until you have written the word, then check your response immediately. If you've made an error, erase and try again.

CHAS_____ .... (CHASTI<u>S</u>ING)

EXER_____ .... (EXERCI<u>S</u>ING)

ADVER_____ .... (ADVERTI<u>S</u>ING)

ADV_____ .... (ADVI<u>S</u>ING)

DESP_____ .... (DESPI<u>S</u>ING)

DEV_____ .... (DEVI<u>S</u>ING)

SUPERV_____ .... (SUPERVI<u>S</u>ING)

IMPROV_____ .... (IMPROVI<u>S</u>ING)

SURPR_____ .... (SURPRI<u>S</u>ING)

REV_____ .... (REVI<u>S</u>ING)

Easy enough? Good—but don't skip a single exercise, because every time you look carefully at a word, every time you write it correctly, you're forcing the proper pattern deep into your spelling memory, you're training yourself to develop the kind of reflexive reactions that will make incorrect patterns impossible.

Now write the word that fits each definition. The initial letter is given to jog your thinking. As before, cover each answer, then check immediately.

1. Whip; beat

   (C-) .... (CHAST*ISE*)

2. Astonish; catch unawares

   (S-) .... (SURPR*ISE*)

3. Make up on the spur of
   the moment

   (I-) .... (IMPROV*ISE*)

4. Give advice to

   (A-) .... (ADV*ISE*)

5. Change; redo with changes

   (R-) .... (REV*ISE*)

6. Do calisthenics

   (E-) .... (EXERC*ISE*)

7. Have great contempt for

   (D-) .... (DESP*ISE*)

8. Put a notice in the newspaper

   (A-) .... (ADVERT*ISE*)

9. Direct and manage;
   superintend

   (S-) .... (SUPERV*ISE*)

10. Figure out; invent

(D-) .... (DEV<u>I</u>SE)

You're really making firm contact with these words. You're looking at them analytically, working with them, writing them in meaningful situations. How many of the ten can you think of without further reference to the original list? Write them as they occur to you, in any order, then glance back at the original list to catch any you missed. But don't give up too easily.

1. .... 6. ....

2. .... 7. ....

3. .... 8. ....

4. .... 9. ....

5. .... 10. ....

Let's Find a Rule

Rules are splendid—if they're so simple they needn't be memorized, and if you already know how to spell the words they cover. <u>A serviceable rule keeps you in close contact with the correct patterns of difficult words—and the best rule is one you try to figure out for yourself.</u> So consider, once again, the following five words—do you see one thing common to all of them?

1. ADV<u>I</u>SE   2. DEV<u>I</u>SE   3. IMPROV<u>I</u>SE
4. REV<u>I</u>SE   5. SUPERV<u>I</u>SE

Got an idea, now? Then write a rule in the space below.

....

....

....

If you're good at finding rules, your answer will say something like this:

> *After the letter V, only -ISE, never -IZE, is used.*

Slippery Letters

Because everyday pronunciation does not exactly indicate the spelling, SURPRISE has an additional pitfall besides the -ISE ending; so do DEVISE and DESPISE. So try these words once again, concentrating this time on the newly underlined areas.

SURPRISE   ....

DEVISE   ....

DESPISE   ....

Chapter **3.**

WORDS WITH CLEARLY DEFINED PARTS

In some (unfortunately, not all) English words, the parts fit together as simply and snugly as the pieces of a child's jigsaw puzzle.

1. Consider a *stand* where *news*papers are sold. If you combine NEWS and STAND into a single word, will there be one S or two?

   □ ONE   □ TWO   (TWO)

   Write the word:

   ....   (NEWS**S**TAND)

2. How about the employee whose function it is to keep the financial records of a business concern? He's a KEEPER of the BOOKS—and if we combine BOOK and KEEPER, how many K's will we use?

   □ ONE   □ TWO   (TWO)

   Write the word:

   ....   (BOO**KK**EEPER)

3. How do we make a noun out of the adjective *clever*? By adding the standard suffix -NESS: *cleverness*. In similar fashion, *vicious* becomes *viciousness; bashful, bashfulness; aggressive, aggressiveness*. And so on. Note, please, that the adjective is not tampered with in any way—not a single letter is dropped, added, or changed before -NESS is tacked on. Therefore, if we attach

-NESS to the adjective SUDDEN, will we have a single
or a double N?

☐ SINGLE ☐ DOUBLE   (DOUBLE)

Write the word:

....   (SUDDE<u>NN</u>ESS)

4. DRUNKEN, rather than *drunk*, is the adjective form
that commonly precedes a noun—a *drunken* sailor, a
drunken bum, a *drunken* orgy, *drunken* drivers. (*Drunk*
usually follows the verb: He got *drunk*. Is he *drunk*?
He was so *drunk* he was almost paralyzed.)

To form the noun, we use the longer adjective,
DRUNKEN, adding, as before, -NESS. How many N's
altogether in the word, then, counting the one before
the K?

☐ TWO ☐ THREE   (THREE)

Write the word:

....   (DRUNKE<u>NN</u>ESS)

5. Now let's form some adverbs. The standard ending, as
you know, is -LY. *Private* becomes *privately*, *warm*
becomes *warmly*, *uneven* becomes *unevenly*. That's easy
enough—merely add -LY.

What if the adjective already ends in L? No difference—still add -LY: *real—really; royal—royally; beautiful—beautifully*. Exactly the same process.

So, therefore, if we want the adverbial form of the
adjective COOL, how many L's will appear in the final
result?

☐ ONE ☐ TWO   (TWO)

Write the word:

....   (COO<u>LL</u>Y)

6. Merely add -LY to the adjective—drop nothing, change
nothing. Suppose the adjective ends in E? Again, no dif-

ference. *Severe—severely; mere—merely; bare—barely; sole—solely.*

Therefore, when we add -LY to the adjective SIN-CERE, is final E dropped or retained?

☐ DROPPED   ☐ RETAINED   (RETAINED)

Write the word:

....   (SINCERELY)

7. The prefix DIS- is attached to the front of a word to make it negative, thus: *like—dislike; pleasure—displeasure; arrange—disarrange; agree—disagree.* Note, if you will, that the prefix is DIS-, not *diss-*.

Now take the verb APPEAR, rarely if ever misspelled. If we make it negative by adding DIS-, how many S's and P's will we have?

☐ S   ☐ P   (one S, two P's)

Write the word:

....   (DISAPPEAR)

8. Another negative prefix is MIS-, as in *misunderstand, misapply, misconstrue, misinterpret,* etc.

Note, once again, that we neatly fit together two parts in each of the words listed: MIS- and *understand;* MIS- and *apply;* MIS- and *construe;* etc.

If, therefore, we want to make SPELLING negative by prefixing MIS-, how many S's will we use?

☐ ONE   ☐ TWO   (TWO)

Write the word:

....   (MISSPELLING)

9. Let us, finally, turn verbs into nouns, a process some-times accomplished by adding the suffix -MENT: *establish—establishment; govern—government; adorn—adornment; advertise—advertisement.* It's as clear-cut

as taking two blocks of wood and nailing one to the other.

So, if we turn the verb DEVELOP into a noun by adding -MENT, will an E follow the P?

□ YES   □ NO   (NO)

Write the word:

....   (DEVELO<u>P</u>MENT)

Step by step, then, we have figured out the correct spelling of nine troublesome and frequently misspelled words. We have seen how component elements form an honest whole, how neatly parts fit together.

Let us look at these words once again, noting where the joints are and thus avoiding any temptation to put extra letters in or leave important letters out. After examining each one, cover it and write it in the blank provided.

NEWS/STAND   ....

BOOK/KEEPER   ....

SUDDEN/NESS   ....

SINCERE/LY   ....

DIS/APPEAR   ....

MIS/SPELLING   ....

DRUNKEN/NESS   ....

COOL/LY   ....

DEVELOP/MENT   ....

Ready for some more practice?

Write the noun form of *develop*.

....   (DEVELO<u>P</u>MENT)

Write the noun form of *drunk*.

....   (DRUNKENNESS)

Write the noun form of *sudden*.

....   (SUDDENNESS)

Write the adverbial form of *sincere*.

....   (SINCERELY)

Write the adverbial form of *cool*.

....   (COOLLY)

Write the opposite of *appear*.

....   (DISAPPEAR)

Write the opposite of *correct spelling*.

....   (MISSPELLING)

On what kind of stand are newspapers
displayed?

....   (NEWSSTAND)

Who keeps the books in a business office?

....   (BOOKKEEPER)

In English spelling it is the rare rule that is not riddled
with exceptions. Not all words are made up of such clearly
separate parts as the nine we have studied—often letters
do have to be dropped or added. But let us reserve those
troubles for a later chapter, concentrating today on important words which follow the rule that the whole is no
more nor less than the sum of two parts. Remembering
how we put our original nine words together, try the following:

1. By adding -NESS, write the noun form of *stubborn*.

   ....   (STUBBOR<u>NN</u>ESS)

2. By adding -LY, write the adverbial form of *lone*.

   ....   (LON<u>EL</u>Y)

3. Similarly, write the adverbial form of *especial*.

   ....   (ESPECIA<u>LL</u>Y)

4. The adverbial form of *real*.

   ....   (REA<u>LL</u>Y)

5. The adverbial form of *accidental*.

   ....   (ACCIDENTA<u>LL</u>Y)

6. The adverbial form of *coincidental*.

   ....   (COINCIDENTA<u>LL</u>Y)

7. The adverbial form of *incidental*.

   ....   (INCIDENTA<u>LL</u>Y)

8. By prefixing DIS-, make *satisfy* negative.

   ....   (DI<u>SS</u>ATISFY)

9. Do the same for *similar*.

   ....   (DI<u>SS</u>IMILAR)

10. And the same for *approve*.

    ....   (DIS<u>AP</u>PROVE)

11. Prefixing DIS- to the verb *appoint*, what
    word do you get?

    ....   (DIS<u>AP</u>POINT)

12. By prefixing MIS-, make the verb *state* negative.

....   (MISSTATE)

13. Make *step* negative in the same way.

....   (MISSTEP)

14. Similarly, make *shape* negative.

....   (MISSHAPE)

15. By adding -MENT, make *embarrass* into a noun.

....   (EMBARRASSMENT)

16. Do the same for the verb *envelop*.

....   (ENVELOPMENT)

17. And, again, for *equip*.

....   (EQUIPMENT)

Following the principle that the whole is merely the sum of two parts, we have had a first crack at writing correctly 17 additional words which are often misspelled.

Note, once again, where the joint occurs, then cover each word with your card and write it correctly.

STUBBORN/NESS	....
LONE/LY	....
ESPECIAL/LY	....
REAL/LY	....
ACCIDENTAL/LY	....
COINCIDENTAL/LY	....
INCIDENTAL/LY	....
DIS/SATISFY	....

DIS/SIMILAR   ....

DIS/APPROVE   ....

DIS/APPOINT   ....

MIS/STATE   ....

MIS/STEP   ....

MIS/SHAPE   ....

EMBARRASS/MENT   ....

ENVELOP/MENT   ....

EQUIP/MENT   ....

Guarding Against Danger Areas

In perfecting your spelling, as I have said, you are for a time alert to the particular place in certain words where most people are likely to fall into a trap. (Eventually, by continuous and meaningful practice, you are able to ignore these traps without even thinking.) Let us examine the pitfalls in the first nine words that we must be especially wary of.

1. NEWSSTAND—the double S.
2. BOOKKEEPER—the double K.
3. SUDDENNESS—the double N.
4. DRUNKENNESS—the double N.
5. COOLLY—the double L.
6. SINCERELY—the E preceding -LY.
7. DISAPPEAR—one S, double P.
8. MISSPELLING—the double S.
9. DEVELOPMENT—no E preceding -MENT.

Do you follow what we're doing here? In each instance, the proper combination of parts produces a word in which the common error is successfully avoided. So, since you have yourself properly combined the parts of the 17 later words, you should now be able to detect and describe the danger area in each one. Try it.

STUBBORNNESS

.... (double N)

LONELY

.... (E before -LY)

ESPECIALLY

.... (double L)

REALLY

.... (double L)

ACCIDENTALLY

.... (double L)

COINCIDENTALLY

.... (double L)

INCIDENTALLY

.... (double L)

DISSATISFY

.... (double S)

DISSIMILAR

.... (double S)

DISAPPROVE (two areas)

.... (single S, double P)

DISAPPOINT (two areas)

.......:........................... (single S, double P)

MISSTATE

.... (double S)

MISSTEP

.... (double S)

MISSHAPE

.... (double S)

EMBARRASSMENT

.... (no E before -MENT)

ENVELOPMENT

.... (no E before -MENT)

EQUIPMENT

.... (no E before -MENT)

By now you have a strong enough visual and muscular memory of each word not to be confused by the incorrect spelling. *Every word below is misspelled*—can you rewrite it correctly?

newstand

.... (NEW**SS**TAND)

bookeeper

.... (BOO**KK**EEPER)

suddeness

.... (SUDDE**NN**ESS)

drunkeness

.... (DRUNKE<u>N</u>NESS)

cooly

.... (COO<u>LL</u>Y)

sincerly

.... (SINCER<u>E</u>LY)

dissapear

.... (DI<u>S</u>A<u>P</u>PEAR)

mispelling

.... (MI<u>S</u>SPELLING)

developement

.... (DEVELO<u>P</u>MENT)

stubborness

.... (STUBBOR<u>N</u>NESS)

lonly

.... (LON<u>E</u>LY)

especialy

.... (ESPECIA<u>LL</u>Y)

realy

.... (REA<u>LL</u>Y)

accidently

.... (ACCIDENTA<u>LL</u>Y) coincidently

.... (COINCIDENT<u>ALL</u>Y)

incidently

.... (INCIDENT<u>ALL</u>Y)

disatisfy

.... (DI<u>SS</u>ATISFY)

disimilar

.... (DI<u>SS</u>IMILAR)

dissaprove

.... (DIS<u>APP</u>ROVE)

dissapoint

.... (DI<u>S</u>A<u>PP</u>OINT)

mistate

.... (MI<u>SS</u>TATE)

mistep

.... (MI<u>SS</u>TEP)

mishape

.... (MI<u>SS</u>HAPE)

embarrasement

.... (EMBA<u>RR</u>A<u>SS</u>MENT)

envelopement

.... (ENVEL<u>OPM</u>ENT)

equipement

.... (EQUIP**M**ENT)

If you have worked at this chapter faithfully, it should be almost impossible for you to misspell a single one of the 26 demons with which you have grappled today.

Let's put it to a final test. Write the word that fits each definition, using the initial letter in parentheses to jog your thinking. As usual, check immediately after each response —if, although it is unlikely, you find that an error persists, erase and try again.

Where newspapers are sold

(N-) ....   (NEW**SS**TAND)

Who makes up the payroll

(B-) ....   (BOO**KK**EEPER)

Unexpectedness

(S-) ....   (SUDDE**NN**ESS)

Intoxication

(D-) ....   (DRUNKE**NN**ESS)

In a cool or calm manner

(C-) ....   (COO**LL**Y)

Honestly; wholeheartedly

(S-) ....   (SINCER**E**LY)

Vanish

(D-) ....   (DIS**APP**EAR)

Incorrect spelling

(M-) ....   (MI**SS**PELLING)

Process of developing

(D-) .... (DEVELOPMENT)

Friendless; alone; deserted

(L-) .... (LONELY)

Obstinacy

(S-) .... (STUBBORNNESS)

Particularly

(E-) .... (ESPECIALLY)

Actually

(R-) .... (REALLY)

By accident

(A-) .... (ACCIDENTALLY)

By coincidence

(C-) .... (COINCIDENTALLY)

By the way

(I-) .... (INCIDENTALLY)

Make unsatisfied

(D-) .... (DISSATISFY)

Not similar

(D-) .... (DISSIMILAR)

Not approve

(D-) .... (DISAPPROVE)

No doubt you have written something like the following:

The letter C, or, *an immediately preceding C.*

And that's all there is to it—directly after the letter C, -EI is used, not -IE.

(The rule applies when the C is pronounced like an S, as it is in all our words for today. When it is pronounced SH, as in *ancient, efficient, sufficient, deficient*, etc., the rule does not, as you can see, apply.)

<u>Always -EI directly after C?</u> Yes, with only one exception, which practically no one misspells: *financier.*

Let's Practice

Which of the nine words we have thus far discussed will properly substitute for the meaning in parentheses in each of the following sentences? Some form of the words other than those listed before may be required, so look sharp. The initial letter will serve to prod your memory.

He is the most (self-admiring) person

I've ever met.

(C-) ....   (CON<u>CEI</u>TED)

He gave me a (paper acknowledging

payment).

(R-) ....   (RE<u>CEI</u>PT)

He makes a habit of (fooling)

people.

(D-) ....   (DE<u>CEI</u>VING)

I can't (get a mental picture)

of such a thing.

(C-) ....   (CON<u>CEI</u>VE)

The (top of the room) was

painted white.

(C-) ....   (CEILING)

Can you (see) any differences
between the twins?

(P-) ....   (PERCEIVE)

He is very (full of a tendency
to lie and cheat).

(D-) ....   (DECEITFUL)

When did you (get possession
of) this?

(R-) ....   (RECEIVE)

He is a (person who deals in
money).

(F-) ....   (FINANCIER)

Remember, then, that:

1. In long E syllables, if the letter C is pronounced S, it is
   followed by -EI, *not* -IE (*receive, conceit*, etc.).
2. The exception is *financier*.
3. When C is pronounced SH, it is followed by -IE (*ancient, efficient*, etc.).
4. Otherwise, in long E syllables, -IE is the likely pattern (*relieve, field, niece*, etc.).

More Practice

Keeping these four points in mind, insert either -IE or -EI
in the blanks below, then rewrite each complete word.

DEC__VER

....   (DECEIVER)

ACH__VE

....   (ACHIEVE)

BR__F

.... (BRIEF)

REC__VE

.... (RECEIVE)

F__LD

.... (FIELD)

GR__F

.... (GRIEF)

GR__VE

.... (GRIEVE)

N__CE

.... (NIECE)

TH__F

.... (THIEF)

W__LD

.... (WIELD)

CONC__T

.... (CONCEIT)

ANC__NT

.... (ANCIENT)

SH__LD

.... (SHIELD)

P__CE

.... (PIECE)

REL__VE

....   (RELIEVE)

Y__LD

....   (YIELD)

REC__VING

....   (RECEIVING)

EFFIC__NT

....   (EFFICIENT)

BEL__VE

....   (BELIEVE)

OMNISC__NT

....   (OMNISCIENT)

SHR__K

....   (SHRIEK)

F__RCE

....   (FIERCE)

REC__PT

....   (RECEIPT)

SUFFIC__NT

....   (SUFFICIENT)

PERC__VE

....   (PERCEIVE)

DEC__T

....   (DECEIT)

PR__ST

....   (PRIEST)

P__R

....   (PIER)

DEC__TFUL

....   (DECEITFUL)

INEFFIC__NT

....   (INEFFICIENT)

CONC__VE

....   (CONCEIVE)

M__N

....   (MIEN)

FINANC__R

....   (FINANCIER)

S__GE

....   (SIEGE)

PERC__VABLE

....   (PERCEIVABLE)

BES__GE

....   (BESIEGE)

CONC__VED

....   (CONCEIVED)

REL__F

....   (RELIEF)

PROFIC__NT

....   (PROFICIENT)

HYG__NE

....   (HYGIENE)

AGGR__VED

....   (AGGRIEVED)

INCONC__VABLE

....   (INCONCEIVABLE)

GR__VOUS

....   (GRIEVOUS)

DEC__VING

....   (DECEIVING)

DEFIC__NT

....   (DEFICIENT)

REC__VER

....   (RECEIVER)

C__LING

....   (CEILING)

CONC__TED

....   (CONCEITED)

Something to Think About

Are there any words with the long E sound that are spelled
-EI even though there is *no* immediately preceding C?

Chapter 5.

MORE ON -IE AND -EI

So—

What have we discovered?

That the letter C is regularly followed by -EI, *not* -IE, in syllables that have the long E sound, as in *ceiling, deceit, receive,* etc.

(But we will bear in mind that *financier* is the one notable exception.)

Are there other words in which -EI is used for the long E sound, even if the preceding letter is *not* C?

There are—quite a number of them. *Either* and *neither* spring immediately to mind (there are those who prefer to say EYE-ther and NEYE-ther, which is a privilege we can't deny them), but these are rarely, if ever, misspelled. There are the verb *seize* and its noun *seizure*—both -EI, even though the preceding letter is S, not C. (These words are so spelled because they derive from Old French *seisir*.) However, don't let *seize* confuse you about *siege* and *besiege,* which regularly follow the rule that it's -IE if there's no preceding C.

In addition to *seize* and *seizure,* there's *leisure* (again from an Old French word, *leisir*), which some people insist on pronouncing LEZH-er, generally those who have enough money to have more of it than they can successfully handle.

And there's *sheik* (also, though no longer commonly, spelled *sheikh*), the chief of an Arab village. And the adjective *weird;* as well as the noun *weir,* a kind of river dam; and the verb *inveigle* (some say in-VEE-gle, some in-VAY-gle), to trick into doing something.

Either, neither, seize, seizure, leisure, sheik, weird, weir, inveigle—all -EI with the sound of long E, even though there's no preceding C.

Also, there are three terms from chemistry—*caffeine*, the alkaloid present in coffee and tea; *codeine*, a derivative of opium; and *protein*, that constituent of meats, fish, eggs, and other foods so necessary for bodily growth and repair.

And what about names? Consider *Keith* and *Neil* and *Sheila* and *Deirdre*, all with at least a slight Irish flavor. Not at all Irish is *Hygeia*, Greek goddess of health (though you will recall that *hygiene*, a related word, is spelled -IE).

In last names we have *Reid*, *O'Neill*, *Goldstein*, and *Rothstein*, the latter two sometimes pronounced with a long I.

(*Freid* and *Freidman* can be spelled EI, but most people with these names prefer *Fried* and *Friedman*. And *Siegfried*, of German mythology, is -IE in both syllables—as is also the *Siegfried line*, built between Germany and France in the 1930's.)

All in all, what does this add up to?

A number of important words violate our rule—they're -EI in long E syllables without a preceding C. People's names, three terms from chemistry, and a few others having no particular relationship among them. Let's get to work on the 11 that are most often misspelled.

Examine each word carefully, taking an accurate mental photograph, and noting especially the -EI combination. Then cover it with the card and rewrite it in the blank.

1. SEIZE   ....

2. SEIZURE   ....

3. INVEIGLE   ....

4. CAFFEINE   ....

5. LEISURE   ....

6. SHEIK   ....

7. WEIRD   ....

8. WEIR ....

9. CODEINE ....

10. PROTEIN ....

11. HYGEIA ....

Have these words made a sufficient impact on you by now? Let us put it to a test. Below are 20 problems—in some -EI is needed, in others -IE. Decide which is which, fill in the blanks, then rewrite the complete word.

1. S__ZE .... (EI)

2. CH__F .... (IE)

3. HYG__A .... (EI)

4. W__RD .... (EI)

5. ACH__VE .... (IE)

6. INV__GLE .... (EI)

7. GR__F .... (IE)

8. BEL__VE .... (IE)

9. SH__K .... (EI)

10. REC__VE .... (EI)

11. CAFF__NE .... (EI)

12. S__GE .... (IE)

13. PROT__N .... (EI)

14. BES__GE .... (IE)

15. L__SURE .... (EI)

16. HYG__NE .... (IE)

17. COD__NE .... (EI)

18. SHR__K .... (IE)

19. W__R   .... (EI)
20. S__ZURE   .... (EI)

Now write the word we've studied that fits each of the following definitions. Initial letters are provided to jog your thinking.

1. Greek goddess

   (H-) ....   (HYGEIA)

2. Grasp; take hold of

   (S-) ....   (SEIZE)

3. An element in food

   (P-) ....   (PROTEIN)

4. Arab chieftain

   (S-) ....   (SHEIK)

5. Element in coffee

   (C-) ....   (CAFFEINE)

6. Time off

   (L-) ....   (LEISURE)

7. Trick into

   (I-) ....   (INVEIGLE)

8. Derivative of opium

   (C-) ....   (CODEINE)

9. A fit; act of grasping

   (S-) ....   (SEIZURE)

10. River dam

   (W-) ....   (WE<u>I</u>R)

11. Eerie, ghostly, uncanny

   (W-) ....   (WE<u>I</u>RD)

Last Chance to Practice

Can you now remember all 11 words we have studied? See how many you can fill in below in any order, without referring to previous material—check back only as a last resort.

1. ....   7. ....

2. ....   8. ....

3. ....   9. ....

4. ....   10. ....

5. ....   11. ....

6. ....

A Problem for Tomorrow

Can you think of some other words spelled -EI in a syllable *not* pronounced long E? Write at least five below.

1. ....   4. ....

2. ....   5. ....

3. ....

Chapter 6.

AND STILL MORE ON -IE, -EI

So we are gradually unraveling -IE and -EI.

We have dealt thus far with syllables in which -EI or -IE has more or less the sound of long E, as in *field, ceiling, leisure*, etc.

What if the combination has the sound of long A, as in *neighbor, freight,* or *weigh*? Do we then always use -EI?

We do. Always.

No exceptions? None.

This is one of the pleasantest and easiest of the patterns of English spelling—if the sound is long A, spell the word -EI, never -IE.

Here is a representative listing of the words so sounded and so spelled. We needn't make a big deal of this, since such words are no major stumbling block for the average speller. Look at each one, say it aloud, then cover it with your card and rewrite it in the blank.

1. WEIGHT ....

2. WEIGH ....

3. REIGN ....

4. DEIGN ....

5. NEIGHBOR ....

6. NEIGH ....

7. FEIGN ....

8. FREIGHT ....

9. SLEIGH ....

10. REINDEER   ....

11. SKEIN   ....

12. REIN   ....

13. VEIN   ....

14. VEIL   ....

There are other words, some of them not quite so common as those above, which have the long A sound and are spelled -EI. Again, study, pronounce, cover, and rewrite.

15. HEINOUS   ....
Extremely wicked, outrageous, as a HEINOUS act, crime, lie, etc.

16. INVEIGH   ....
To make a strong attack in words. Always followed by *against*, as in *The speaker INVEIGHED against war, crime, his enemies*, etc.

17. INVEIGLE   ....
To entice or trick into something, as *He INVEIGLED me into signing the contract*. (Some people say in-VAY-gle, others in-VEE-gle. However you pronounce it, you spell it -EI.)

18. CHOW MEIN   ....
A popular Chinese dish. The second part of the word is pronounced MAYN, and should not be confused with *mien* (one's bearing, manner, or air), which is pronounced MEEN and spelled -IE.

19. SEINE   ....
A large fishing net. Identical in pronunciation with the adjective *sane*. Use a capital S and you have the French river, most famous perhaps for its left bank.

20. SEICHE   ....
The rhythmical, side-to-side movement of the waters of a lake. Pronounced SAYSH.

More Words for Today

-EI, then, follows C (except for FINANCIER).

It is found in such exceptions as WEIRD, LEISURE, SEIZE, etc.

It occurs when the sound of the syllable is long A, as in WEIGH, REIN, etc.

Where else does it occur?

Consider these words, noting the sound of -EI in each. As before, study, pronounce, cover, and rewrite.

21. FAHRENHEIT   ....
    The temperature scale widely used in the U. S. Pronounced FĂR-en-HITE, the first syllable rhyming with the *car-* of *carriage.*

22. GNEISS   ....
    A kind of rock. Identical in pronunciation with the adjective *nice,* the G being totally silent.

23. HEIGHT   ....
    Pronounced HITE.

24. LEITMOTIV   ....
    A recurring musical phrase in an opera. Pronounced LITE-mo-TEEF.

25. SEISMIC   ....
    Referring to earthquakes. Pronounced SIZE-mik.

26. SLEIGHT OF HAND   ....
    The first word is pronounced SLITE.

27. STEIN   ....
    A mug for beer. Pronounced STINE.

28. SEIDEL   ....
    Another beer mug, usually with a hinged lid. Pronounced SYE-d'l.

FAHRENHEIT, GNEISS, HEIGHT, LEITMOTIV, SEISMIC, SLEIGHT OF HAND, STEIN, SEIDEL—all

-EI, and in every instance the syllable containing -EI is pronounced long I, that is, like the word *eye*.

Are all long I syllables spelled -EI rather than -IE? Yes —unless the next letter is R; but we'll tackle those in the next chapter.

Here again are the eight words we've just discussed. Look at each, say it aloud, then cover it with your card and rewrite it.

FAHRENHEIT ....

GNEISS ....

HEIGHT ....

LEITMOTIV ....

SEISMIC ....

STEIN ....

SLEIGHT (OF HAND) ....

SEIDEL ....

Still More Words for Today

We've spoken of the sound of long E (LEISURE, RE-CEIVE); long A (WEIGHT, FREIGHT); and long I (HEIGHT, STEIN).

What if the vowel sound of a syllable is not long, and is so slightly sounded as to be obscure, as the I in *devil?*

Note in the two groups of words below that -EI has a very obscure sound. You can discover, without too much trouble, what is common to the words of each group.

GROUP I	GROUP II
29. FORFEIT	32. FOREIGN
30. SURFEIT	33. FOREIGNER
31. COUNTERFEIT	34. SOVEREIGN
	35. SOVEREIGNTY

The common element in Group I is the -FEIT ending; in Group II the -GN following EI-.

So in slightly sounded syllables we use -EI in -FEIT syllables, or if followed by -GN.

Do we use -EI in any other short syllables?

Yes, in three special words in which the combination is pronounced short E, as in *well* or *bell*.

36. HEIFER ....
    A young cow. Pronounced HEFF-er.

37. NONPAREIL ....
    Unequaled, matchless, peerless, etc. Pronounced non-pa-RELL.

38. SEIDLITZ ....
    A kind of effervescing powder used as a laxative or to settle the stomach. Pronounced SED-litz.

Otherwise, as we shall discover, in the next chapter, short syllables are generally written with -IE not -EI.

Look again at each of our new words, say it aloud, cover it up, then rewrite it.

FORFEIT   ....

SURFEIT   ....

COUNTERFEIT   ....

FOREIGN   ....

FOREIGNER   ....

SOVEREIGN   ....

SOVEREIGNTY   ....

HEIFER   ....

NONPAREIL   ....

SEIDLITZ   ....

Run-Down on -EI Rules

The best, and quickest, way to understand and remember a spelling rule is to discover how all the examples fit into a pattern.

Examining the details and gradually uncovering a general principle is *creative* learning. Blindly memorizing the rule and then applying it to individual words is by contrast so mechanical and passive that the learning is far less effective, much more likely to be impermanent.

In this and in the two preceding chapters, you have examined, worked with, and practiced on, various groups of -EI words. You've then shared in the discovery of the rule that covers each group.

Remember, words are not spelled in certain patterns because the rule says they should be. Rather, the rule *generalizes* on the occurrence of patterns.

So let us put all our conclusions about -EI words in one place. Every statement you read below will touch a memory nerve, will recall to you what you already know.

1. In long E syllables, -EI is used after C.
   Write four examples.

   ....

   ....

   Write one exception (-IE after C).

   ....

2. A number of important exceptions, still pronounced long E, are spelled -EI even though there is no immediately preceding C.
   Write five examples.

   ....

   ....

   ....

3. In long A syllables, all words are spelled -EI, not -IE.
   Write four examples.

   ....

   ....

4. In long I syllables, most words are spelled -EI, not -IE.
   Write two examples.

   ....

5. In slightly sounded syllables, -EI is used in -FEIT and
   -EIGN combinations.
   Write two examples of each.

   ....

   ....

6. Finally, there are three special words which are spelled
   -EI in syllables pronounced with a short E sound.
   Write two of them.

   ....

This run-down is a complete review of what you have
learned in chapters 4, 5, and 6. If you had any trouble
thinking of the examples asked for, go back to the text of
these chapters and find what's missing.

Preview for Tomorrow

We've discussed -IE in long E syllables: BELIEVE,
NIECE, RETRIEVE, etc. Can you, now, think of five
words in which -IE is used in syllables that have a short I
or obscure vowel sound? Here are two to get you started:
HANDKERCHIEF, ANCIENT.

Chapter 7.

FINAL MOP-UP ON -IE, -EI

Now let us nail down the last remaining principles on -IE, -EI.

You know that -IE, not -EI, is used on long E syllables in which there is no immediately preceding C.

Examples are FIELD, PRIEST, RELIEVE, ACHIEVE, and so on.

What about syllables which are pronounced either with an obscure vowel sound or with the short I of *hit* or *bit?* You already know that -EI is used in -EIT and -EIGN combinations. *For other obscure or short vowel sounds we use -IE.* Let's see whether you can discover some of these for yourself.

I. Can you think of three words in which -IE follows the letters CH- ? The definition and initial letter will jog your thinking.

1. A cloth carried in the pocket

(H-) .... (HANDKERCHIEF)

2. Naughtiness, playful pranks

(M-) .... (MISCHIEF)

3. The adjective form of the preceding word

(M-) .... (MISCHIEVOUS)

II. Can you think of -IE words in which C has the sound of SH? They all end in *-cient.*

4. Very old

   (A-) .... (ANCIENT)

5. One's inner voice that controls behavior

   (C-) .... (CONSCIENCE)

6. Lacking

   (D-) .... (DEFICIENT)

7. Competent

   (E-) .... (EFFICIENT)

8. All-knowing

   (O-) .... (OMNISCIENT)

9. Extremely capable, skilled

   (P-) .... (PROFICIENT)

10. Having an awareness of future events

    (P-) .... (PRESCIENT)

11. Enough

    (S-) .... (SUFFICIENT)

III. Can you think of some additional words in which -IE has the obscure vowel sound? All of the following end in -IENT.

12. Willing to wait calmly; as a noun, one who visits a doctor

    (P-) .... (PATIENT)

13. The opposite of word 12.

    (I-) .... (IMPATIENT)

14. The result when one number is divided
    by another

    (Q-) ....   (QUOTIENT)

15. What word beginning with S means a strainer or filter?

    ....   (SIEVE)

16. What word beginning with F means a companion or
    buddy?

    ....   (FRIEND)

    Can you think of at least three derivatives of this word?

    .... (FRIENDLY,

    ....FRIENDSHIP,

    ....UNFRIENDLY,

    ....BEFRIEND, etc.)

If you were able to think of most of these words before
checking with the answers, excellent! To spell a word correctly in a meaningful situation is far more productive of
lasting learning than mere mechanical copying.

So let us finish with another exercise in which you try
to discover by yourself the words on which you will practice.

Most words in which a syllable is pronounced with the
sound of long I, we decided in the previous chapter, will be
spelled -EI rather than -IE. Examples, you will remember,
were HEIGHT, SEISMIC, STEIN, etc.

But three common words with almost this long I sound
are spelled -IE—and in each instance the next letter is R.
Can you think of them?

17. Full of, or like, fire; vehement,
    spirited, high-tempered

    (F-)   ....   (FIERY)

18. Group of officials or ruling persons
    considered in order of rank

    (H-)   ....   (HIERARCHY)

19. Symbol in ancient Egyptian writing

    (H-)   ....   (HIEROGLYPHIC)

(There are a few others in which -IE is followed by R, but they are rather abstruse. For example, *hieratic, hierocracy, hierology, hierophant,* etc.)

Run-Down on -IE Rules

The correct combination, then, is -IE:

1. In long E syllables except after C, for instance BE-LIEVE. Can you think of four more examples?

   ....

   ....

2. In most obscure or short I syllables, for instance SIEVE. Can you think of four more examples?

   ....

   ....

3. In long I syllables when the next letter is R, for instance HIERARCHY. Can you think of two further examples?

   ....

4. In the word FRIEND and all its derivatives. Can you think of two such derivatives?

....

Words for Today

Another quick look at these words, now, with a chance to write each one. Examine the pattern carefully, cover the word with your card, then write it correctly in the blank.

HANDKERCHIEF   ....

KERCHIEF   ....

MISCHIEF   ....

MISCHIEVOUS   ....

ANCIENT   ....

CONSCIENCE   ....

DEFICIENT   ....

EFFICIENT   ....

OMNISCIENT   ....

PROFICIENT   ....

PRESCIENT   ....

SUFFICIENT   ....

PATIENT   ....

IMPATIENT   ....

QUOTIENT   ....

SIEVE   ....

FRIEND   ....

FRIENDLY   ....

FRIENDSHIP   ....

UNFRIENDLY   ....

BEFRIEND   ....

FIERY   ....

HIERARCHY   ....

HIEROGLYPHIC   ....

Preview for Tomorrow

The work you have done in the last six chapters aimed to develop in you quick, correct, and completely self-assured responses to the spelling of approximately 140 words offered for learning and practice. In the next chapter we shall test how nearly expert—perhaps even infallible—you have become.

Chapter 8.
FIRST REVIEW TEST

I. Of the following 20 verbs, some are spelled correctly, others are deliberately misspelled. If the pattern looks right to you, check the blank. If you detect an error, rewrite the word.

1. sympathize .... (√)

2. utilize .... (√)

3. chastize .... (-ise)

4. exercize .... (-ise)

5. organize .... (√)

6. advize .... (-ise)

7. victimize .... (√)

8. improvize .... (-ise)

9. criticize .... (√)

10. surprize .... (-ise)

11. civilize .... (√)

12. advertize .... (-ise)

13. agonize .... (√)

14. revize .... (-ise)

15. supervize .... (-ise)

16. alphabetize .... (√)

17. devize .... (-ise)

18. despize .... (-ise)

19. economize .... (√)

20. baptize .... (√)

II. Find the *one* misspelled word on each line and rewrite it correctly.

1. newsstand, bookkeeper, developement, equipment.

.... (development)

2. suddenness, drunkeness, stubbornness, barrenness.

.... (drunkenness)

3. sincerely, lonely, really, cooly.

.... (coolly)

4. incidently, accidentally, especially, solely.

.... (incidentally)

5. dissatisfy, dissimilar, dissapoint, disapprove.

.... (disappoint)

6. misspelling, misstate, misstep, mishapen.

.... (misshapen)

III. Of the following words, some are correctly spelled -IE, some -EI. Fill in the proper pattern, then rewrite the word.

1. rec......ve .... (ei)
2. s......zure .... (ei)
3. ch......f .... (ie)
4. w......ld .... (ie)
5. w......ght .... (ei)
6. cod......ne .... (ei)
7. s......ge .... (ie)
8. f......rce .... (ie)
9. h......ght .... (ei)
10. conc......ted .... (ei)
11. bes......ge .... (ie)
12. forf......t .... (ei)
13. w......rd .... (ei)
14. s......ve .... (ie)
15. n......ce .... (ie)
16. inv......gle .... (ei)
17. shr......k .... (ie)
18. dec......t .... (ei)
19. ach......ve .... (ie)
20. misch......vous .... (ie)
21. fr......ndly .... (ie)
22. gr......f .... (ie)
23. y......ld .... (ie)
24. l......sure .... (ei)
25. c......ling .... (ei)

26. f.....ry   .... (ie)

27. for.....gn   .... (ei)

28. suffic.....nt   .... (ie)

29. financ.....r   .... (ie)

30. h.....fer   .... (ei)

31. h.....roglyphic   .... (ie)

32. pr.....st   .... (ie)

33. rel.....ve   .... (ie)

Chapter 9.
DOUBLE L

For the most part, a double consonant in English has the same sound as a single consonant.

Thus, the middle consonant is pronounced identically in *palace* and in *ballot;* in *widow* and in *bedding;* in *Paris* and in *parrot;* in *honor* and in *winner*.

And so, as you might suspect, one of the chief, and most vexing, problems in English spelling is whether or not to double a consonant.

For example, the consonant L. To most people, *vacilate* looks as good as *vacillate, oscilate* as good as *oscillate, scintilate* as good as *scintillate*. And why not? Scores of verbs end in single -LATE: *annihilate, calculate, coagulate, populate, stipulate,* to mention just a few.

But five important, and frequently misspelled, verbs end in double -LATE.

Words for Today—with Practice

Look carefully at each of the verbs below—note, and impress on your visual memory, the double L, then cover the word and rewrite it correctly.

1. OSCILLATE ....
   To swing back and forth like a pendulum.

2. TITILLATE ....
   To stimulate pleasantly. (Note that all the T's are single.)

3. VACILLATE ....
   To waver in indecision. (Note that there is no S before the C.)

4. FLAGE**LL**ATE   ....
   To whip or flog.

5. SCINTI**LL**ATE   ....
   To sparkle with wit.

To conquer words like these, which depart so radically from typical -ATE verbs, your greatest ally is a strong response to their proper appearance. If you practice writing them a few times, concentrating on the double L in each one, you will never again be tempted to misspell them.

More Practice

Write the noun form, ending in -TION, of each verb. The initial is given in parentheses.

Indecision

(V-) ....   (VACI**LL**ATION)

Brilliant display of wit

(S-) ....   (SCINTI**LL**ATION)

Back and forth motion

(O-) ....   (OSCI**LL**ATION)

Act of flogging

(F-) ....   (FLAGE**LL**ATION)

Pleasurable stimulation

(T-) ....   (TITI**LL**ATION)

Once Again, with Feeling

Substitute the -ING form of each verb for the word or words in parentheses.

Certain minor religious sects believe in

(whipping) themselves as a form of
purification.

(F-) .... (FLAGELLATING)

He finds that reading pornographic
books is (pleasantly stimulating).

(T-) .... (TITILLATING)

The weight was (swinging back and
forth) like a pendulum.

(O-) .... (OSCILLATING)

"You were (sparking with wit)
tonight," he told his wife.

(S-) .... (SCINTILLATING)

She was (changing her mind over
and over).

(V-) .... (VACILLATING)

More Words for Today

Let us not waste the strong mind-set you have now developed for double L's. Consider the following words, most of them fairly common, all of them frequently misspelled. Look long and hard at each one, noting where the double L occurs, then cover it and rewrite it correctly.

  6. ALLOTMENT   ....

  7. COLLABORATE   ....

  8. PARALLEL   ....

  9. SATELLITE   ....

10. MISCELLANEOUS   ....

11. ALL RIGHT   ....

12. WILLFUL   ....

13. TRANQUILLITY   ....

14. WOOLLY   ....

15. BALLOON   ....

16. ELLIPSE   ....

17. TONSILLITIS   ....

18. VILLAIN   ....

19. WHOLLY   ....

20. SKILLFUL   ....

21. UNSKILLFUL   ....

22. METALLIC   ....

Seventeen new words—but the unifying theme of the double L makes it possible to assimilate them all, with no difficulty, in a single session.

Incidentally, a few of them (WILLFUL, SKILLFUL, UNSKILLFUL, TRANQUILLITY, and WOOLLY) have variant spellings in which the L is not doubled—but those single L forms, though technically correct, are so infrequently used that it would be best for you to become accustomed to the patterns indicated.

Note, particularly, before you engage in further practice that:

—in PARALLEL, the first L, not the second, is doubled.

—in SATELLITE, though the sound of the word might tempt you to use a double T after the A, only one T is correct.

—though WOOLLY is the form preferable for this adjective, WOOLEN, contradictorily, is preferably spelled with one L.

—in BALLOON, the O is also doubled.

So, Down to Practice

You've written each of our 17 new words once, concentrating on the double L's and relying on your visual memory. Now let's practice in a more meaningful situation. I'll give you the definition and initial letter of each word— can you write it correctly?

Inflatable rubber bag

(B-) .... (BALLOON)

Without skill

(U-) .... (UNSKILLFUL)

O.K.

(A-) .... (ALL RIGHT)

Of various kinds

(M-) .... (MISCELLANEOUS)

Made of, or like, wool

(W-) .... (WOOLLY)

Small planet revolving around a larger one

(S-) .... (SATELLITE)

Work together

(C-) .... (COLLABORATE)

Flattened circle

(E-) .... (ELLIPSE)

One's portion or share

(A-) .... (ALLOTMENT)

Inflammation of the tonsils

(T-) ....   (TONSILLITIS)

Completely

(W-) ....   (WHOLLY)

Calmness; peace

(T-) ....   (TRANQUILLITY)

Running in the same direction,
and always the same distance
apart, as lines, etc.

(P-) ....   (PARALLEL)

Intentional; stubborn; headstrong

(W-) ....   (WILLFUL)

Like metal

(M-) ....   (METALLIC)

Rogue; scoundrel

(V-) ....   (VILLAIN)

Exhibiting skill

(S-) ....   (SKILLFUL)

Final Practice

Ready for the acid test of your learning? Generally it is
unwise for a student to see a misspelling until the correct
pattern is so familiar to him that he is in no danger whatever of being seduced by the improper form. At this point
you should have developed sufficient familiarity with the
22 words we have studied to make you reject, out of hand,
an incorrectly spelled form.

Every word below is either misspelled or deviates from its preferable pattern. Cross it out and rewrite it correctly.

oscilate

....   (OSCILLATE)

tittilate

....   (TITILLATE)

vascilate

....   (VACILLATE)

flaggelate

....   (FLAGELLATE)

scintilate

....   (SCINTILLATE)

alotment

....   (ALLOTMENT)

colaborate

....   (COLLABORATE)

paralell

....   (PARALLEL)

sattelite

....   (SATELLITE)

miscelaneous

....   (MISCELLANEOUS)

alright

....   (ALL RIGHT) tranquility

....   (TRANQUILLITY)

wooly

....   (WOOLLY)

baloon

....   (BALLOON)

elipse

....   (ELLIPSE)

tonsilitis

....   (TONSILLITIS)

vilain

....   (VILLAIN)

wholy

....   (WHOLLY)

skilful

....   (SKILLFUL)

unskilful

....   (UNSKILLFUL)

mettalic

....   (METALLIC)

wilful

....   (WILLFUL)

Problem for Tomorrow

Can you think of any words which have a single consonant
in one form, but the same consonant doubled in a longer
form?

Chapter 10.

DOUBLING A FINAL CONSONANT (I)

Let's work together today and see how easy it is to arrive at some useful spelling rules that prevent you from misspelling scores upon scores of words that cause doubt and confusion to most people. To work successfully, make sure you answer each question in writing.

Start with OCCUR, which almost everyone spells correctly.

How many R's in this verb?

.... (1)

Now write it in the past tense.

.... (OCCURRED)

How many R's this time?

.... (2)

Now add -ING to OCCUR.

.... (OCCURRING)

How many R's now?

.... (2)

Write the noun form of OCCUR, ending in -NCE.

.... (OCCURRENCE)

How many R's now?

.... (2)

We have seen, then, that OCCUR has only one R, but the derived forms OCCURRED, OCCURRING, and OCCURRENCE have double R's.

So let's figure out the rule that can be deduced from all these facts. Again, answer the questions in writing.

OCCUR ends in a single consonant, or in more than one consonant?

....   (single)

This single consonant is immediately preceded by how many vowels—one, or more than one?

....   (one)

In the pronunciation of OCCUR, does the accent fall on the first or on the last syllable?

....   (last)

When we add -ED, -ING, or -ENCE, does each suffix start with a vowel or a consonant?

....   (vowel)

We have decided that the accent on OCCUR falls on the last syllable, that is, on *-cur*. In the words OCCURRED, OCCURRING, and OCCURRENCE, does the accent remain on *-cur*, yes or no?

....   (yes)

That's all there is to what might otherwise be a very complicated rule. Now you know when to double a final consonant before adding a suffix, when not to.

Let's just review it briefly, relying on you to fill in the crucial words.

Keeping OCCUR and suffixes -ED, -ING, and -ENCE in mind, help me formulate the rule.

—If a word ends in a .... consonant,   (single)

—Preceded by a .... vowel   (single)

—And is accented on the .... syllable   (last)

—Double this consonant when adding a suffix

   that starts with a ....,   (vowel)

—Provided the accent .... on what   (remains)

   was the final syllable of the original word.

Now don't bother to memorize this rule—no one is ever likely to ask you to repeat it verbatim. But *understand* it, feel secure about every one of the five parts of it, and you'll never have another problem about doubling, or not doubling, a final consonant when adding a suffix.

Bear in mind that every one of the five clauses has to be operative before the rule applies.

1. *The word must end in just one consonant, not two or more.*

Thus, the rule applies to COMPEL, which ends in the single consonant L, but not to RESIST, which ends in two consonants, S and T. (Therefore, we write COMPELLED and COMPELLING, doubling the L, but RESISTED and RESISTING.)

2. *There must be only one vowel before this final single consonant, not two or more.*

The rule applies, then, to REFER, in which the single vowel E precedes the final consonant R, but not to APPEAR, in which two vowels, E and A, precede the R. (Therefore, we write REFERRED and REFERRING, with a double R, but APPEARED and APPEARING, with only one R.)

3. *The last syllable of the verb must receive the accent.*

In COMMIT, for example, the accent is on -*mit*, the last syllable; in PROFIT, however, the accent is on *prof-*, the first syllable. So we double the final T of COMMIT before adding a suffix that starts with a vowel (COMMITTED, COMMITTING, COMMITTEE); we do not double the final T of PROFIT (PROFITED, PROFITING, PROFITEER).

4. *The suffix to be added must start with a vowel, not a consonant.*

For example, if we add -MENT, which starts with the consonant M, we never double:

> ALLOT—ALLOTMENT
> DEFER—DEFERMENT
> COMMIT—COMMITMENT

However, when we add -ED, which starts with the vowel E, we do double:

> ALLOTTED
> DEFERRED
> COMMITTED

5. *The accent must not shift off what was the final syllable of the original verb.*

For instance, the accent remains on the -cur when OCCUR becomes OCCURRENCE, hence the double R. But the accent shifts back to the first syllable when PREFER becomes PREFERENCE, hence the R is not doubled.

This is not a bit difficult, and, as I have said, you need not memorize the rule, *merely understand it.* Once you do, you will be self-assured on doubling or not doubling with hundreds upon hundreds of verbs to which suffixes are added, most of which are liable to misspelling.

Furthermore, the rule is almost foolproof—the exceptions are so few and so rarely troublesome that we will be perfectly safe in ignoring them for the moment.

Words for Today, with Practice

Now let us see whether you understand how the rule works. Every verb below, as you will notice, ends in a single consonant preceded by a single vowel, is accented on the final syllable, and does not shift its accent when a suffix is added.

Look at each word, note the characteristics that were detailed in the previous paragraph, then rewrite it adding -ED.

1. CONCUR .... (CONCURRED)

2. OCCUR .... (OCCURRED)

3. CONFER .... (CONFERRED)

4. REFER .... (REFERRED)

5. DETER .... (DETERRED)

6. ANNUL .... (ANNULLED)

7. EXPEL .... (EXPELLED)

8. CONTROL.................................... (CONTROLLED)

9. ACQUIT .... (ACQUITTED)

10. COMMIT .... (COMMITTED)

11. OMIT .... (OMITTED)

12. ALLOT .... (ALLOTTED)

13. REGRET .... (REGRETTED)

14. PREFER .... (PREFERRED)

15. COMPEL .... (COMPELLED)

16. EQUIP .... (EQUIPPED)

More Words; More Practice

Consider BENEFIT. It ends in a single consonant, T. The T is preceded by a single vowel, I. *But our rule does not apply to it*, because we say BEN-e-fit, *with the accent on the first syllable, rather than on the final syllable*. Hence, we write BENEFITED, BENEFITING, with one T, not two. Say the following verbs aloud, noting that in each instance the accent does *not* fall on the last syllable. Will you, then, double the final consonant before adding -ED?

☐ YES ☐ NO   (NO)

17. PROHIBIT   .... (PROHIBITED)
18. TRAVEL   .... (TRAVELED)
19. JEWEL   .... (JEWELED)
20. MARVEL   .... (MARVELED)
21. COUNSEL   .... (COUNSELED)
22. SIGNAL   .... (SIGNALED)
23. CANCEL   .... (CANCELED)
24. WALLOP   .... (WALLOPED)
25. WORSHIP   .... (WORSHIPED)
26. ENVELOP   .... (ENVELOPED)
27. MERIT   .... (MERITED)
28. PROFIT   .... (PROFITED)
29. RIVET   .... (RIVETED)

Chapter 11.
DOUBLING A FINAL CONSONANT (II)

Learning involves memory, but it is not simply memorizing—it is not mechanically going over the same thing again and again.

A parrot can "learn" to say a limited number of words—it cannot learn to talk in the full sense of the word; that is, it is not capable of understanding and communicating.

True learning is built on understanding and change that build up a reservoir of permanent memory.

When you really learn a principle of English spelling (whether or not you can quote it exactly) you *understand* how to apply it, you continue applying it until correct patterns become habitual and finally reflexive.

When this point is reached, and it takes less time than you may think, misspellings are impossible.

All that I have said is especially applicable to the many hundreds of words whose patterns are governed by the doubling principle which you worked on in the previous chapter. By now you *understand* when final consonants are, and when they are not, doubled. You have applied the principle in reasonably reacting to, and in writing out, some 30 or so troublesome words.

Today we'll learn nothing particularly new—instead we'll go on applying the recently learned principles to still more words.

Let's Practice

Let us add some new suffixes to words ending in a single consonant preceded by a single vowel.

1. Add -ENT to:

CONCUR .... (CONCURRENT)

DETER   .... (DETERRENT)

RECUR   .... (RECURRENT)

REPEL   .... (REPELLENT)

2. The next suffix to be added is -ENCE.

OCCUR   .... (OCCURRENCE)

RECUR   .... (RECURRENCE)

INCUR   .... (INCURRENCE)

DETER   .... (DETERRENCE)

CONCUR .... (CONCURRENCE)

3. Again add -ENCE, but note this time that the accent in the resulting word will shift back to the first syllable. That will rule out, as you remember, doubling the final syllable.

CONFER   .... (CONFERENCE)

DEFER   .... (DEFERENCE)

INFER   .... (INFERENCE)

PREFER   .... (PREFERENCE)

REFER   .... (REFERENCE)

4. Now add -ING, another suffix starting with a vowel, to the following, all of which, as you will notice, satisfy the requirements of the doubling principle.

EQUIP   .... (EQUIPPING)

EXCEL   .... (EXCELLING)

ALLOT   .... (ALLOTTING)

ANNUL   .... (ANNULLING)

PATROL	.... (PATROLLING)
DISPEL	.... (DISPELLING)
EXPEL	.... (EXPELLING)
ACQUIT	.... (ACQUITTING)
ADMIT	.... (ADMITTING)
REGRET	.... (REGRETTING)

5. Add -MENT, a suffix that starts with a *consonant*, thus violating one of the requirements of the doubling principle.

ANNUL	.... (ANNULMENT)
EQUIP	.... (EQUIPMENT)
COMMIT	.... (COMMITMENT)
DEFER	.... (DEFERMENT)
INTER	.... (INTERMENT)
ALLOT	.... (ALLOTMENT)

6. Add -ING to the following, on which the accent is *not* on the final syllable, thus again violating one of the requirements of the doubling principle.

FOCUS	.... (FOCUSING)
BIAS	.... (BIASING)
KIDNAP	.... (KIDNAPING)
MARVEL	.... (MARVELING)
CANCEL	.... (CANCELING)
LIBEL	.... (LIBELING)
ENVELOP	.... (ENVELOPING)
WORSHIP	.... (WORSHIPING)

7. Finally, add -ER to the same kind of word.

KIDNAP	....	(KIDNAPER)
LIBEL	....	(LIBELER.)
WORSHIP	....	(WORSHIPER)
SUFFER	....	(SUFFERER)
BANQUET	....	(BANQUETER)
PROFIT	....	(PROFITER)
RIVET	....	(RIVETER)

A Note on One-Syllable Words

What if a word satisfies all the requirements of the doubling principle—single consonant, preceding single vowel, suffix starting with a vowel—but contains only one syllable so that no question of accent is involved? *Then, of course, we always double.* Try the following for example, adding the indicated suffix and rewriting the complete word.

sob plus -ED

....   (SOBBED)

run plus -ER

....   (RUNNER)

stop plus -ING

....   (STOPPING)

swim plus -ER

....   (SWIMMER)

bid plus -ING

....   (BIDDING)

beg plus -AR

....   (BEGGAR)

bug plus -Y

....   (BUGGY)

plan plus -ING

....   (PLANNING)

thin plus -EST

....   (THINNEST)

fur plus -Y

....   (FURRY)

quiz plus -ES

....   (QUIZZES)

quiz plus -ED

....   (QUIZZED)

quiz plus -ING

....   (QUIZZING)

Random Notes on the Peculiarities of English Spelling

Some of the words detailed earlier in this chapter in which we did *not* double a final consonant since the accent did *not* fall on the final syllable (*kidnap, cancel, libel,* etc.) have variant spellings, occasionally seen and technically not incorrect, containing a doubled consonant.

Kidnapper, kidnapped, and *kidnapping,* for example, are common; their popularity may be accounted for by the fact that the word is made up of two parts, *kid* and *nap,* which derives from *nab.* Since the P of *nap,* a one-syllable word, is regularly doubled before a suffix (*napped, napping,* etc.), there is a very strong influence to double the P in derived forms of *kidnap.* But the single P spellings are far preferable, and I suggest you follow the rule on this word.

The British tend to double a final consonant even when the accent falls on the first syllable of a word; they would write *marvelled, marvellous, travelled, traveller, jewelled, worshipping,* etc., where we regularly employ a single L or P. It is strongly recommended that you follow the American style. (Oddly enough, *The New Yorker,* a completely American magazine, prefers, for reasons hard to understand, the British form of these and similar words.)

Again following the rule in *program* and *diagram,* each accented on the first syllable, we should not double the M before a vowel suffix—but *programed, programing, diagramed,* and *diagraming* look so strange to most people that the double M forms, also correct, are more popular.

Chagrin is an exception of an opposite kind. The doubling principle should apply, and all sense demands a double N before -ED or -ING—but the only correct, the only allowable, spellings, are *chagrined,* and *chagrining.* There is no way to justify this anomaly—we must simply accept that English is a language in which *beginning* has a double N, and *chagrining,* which rhymes with it, has only one N in the middle.

Quiz appears, at first glance, to end in a single consonant, preceded by *two* vowels (U, I). But the U is pronounced as a W *(kwiz),* and only the I functions as a true vowel. Therefore, the doubling principle very much applies, and the Z is of course doubled before a vowel suffix: *quizzes, quizzed, quizzing, quizzical.* The same holds for *quit, acquit, equip,* and any other QU- combination.

Chapter 12.

DOUBLING A FINAL CONSONANT (III)

Are you ready, now, to nail down permanently your understanding of the fine art of doubling?

Move along with me, pencil at the ready, as I ask you some direct and very detailed questions.

Check each of your answers at once so that every proper response you make will reinforce your learning, and every error or misconception can immediately be corrected.

1. The doubling principle operates when
   we add a ...., such as -ED, -ING,
   -ER, -AL, etc., to a word.   (suffix)

2. The type of word involved in the doubling principle ends in a single

   ....   (consonant)

3. Of the following words, which *one*
   does *not* end in a single consonant:
   remit, grip, begin, invest, occur, excel?   (invest)

4. This single consonant must be pre-
   ceded by a single ....   (vowel)

5. Of the following words, in which *one*
   is the final consonant *not* preceded by
   a single vowel: *kidnap, allot, remain,*
   prefer, forbid?   (remain)

6. Furthermore, the suffix to be added

   must start with a ....   (vowel)

7. Of the following suffixes, which one
   starts with a consonant: -ED, -MENT,
   -ING, -Y?   (-MENT)

8. The words to which the doubling prin-

   ciple applies either have only ....
   syllable . . . ,   (one)

9. Or, if they have two or more syllables,

   receive the accent on the .... syl-
   lable.   (final *or* last)

10. *Hit*, *bar*, *stop*, and *bag* are examples of

    words containing .... syllable.   (one)

11. *Refer*, *admit*, *equip*, and *begin* are ex-
    amples of words that are accented on

    the .... syllable.   (final *or* last)

12. *Travel*, *develop*, *suffer*, and *rivet* are
    examples of words in which the accent

    does *not* fall on the .... syllable.   (final *or* last)

13. If we add -ED to *refer*, then, we □ do,

    □ do not, double the final R.   (do)

14. If we add -ED to *travel*, we □ do,

    □ do not, double the final L.   (do not)

15. *Chagrin* is the kind of word to which
    the doubling principle applies. Con-
    trarily, however, before adding -ED or

    -ING, we □ do, □ do not, double the
    N.   (do not)

16. In the derived forms of *kidnap*, a □

    single, □ double P is preferable.   (single)

17. When final-syllable accent *shifts back*, as when -ENCE is added to *refer*, we ☐ do, ☐ do not, double the R.　　　(do not)

18. When the accent *remains* on the final syllable, as when -ENCE is added to *occur*, we ☐ do, ☐ do not, double the R.　　　(do)

19. If -MENT, a suffix starting with a consonant, is added to one of these words, the final consonant ☐ is, ☐ is not, doubled.　　　(is not)

20. Before adding -MENT to *equip*, ☐ double, ☐ do not double, the final P.　　　(do not)

21. Before adding -ED, to *equip*, ☐ double, ☐ do not double, final P.　　　(double)

22. Before adding -ED to *worship*, ☐ dou-. ble, ☐ do not double, final P.　　　(do not)

23. -Y as a suffix is considered a vowel. Before adding -Y to *bug*, ☐ double, ☐ do not double, final G.　　　(double)

24. The letter -U in QU- combinations is considered a consonant since it has the sound of ....　　　(W)

25. Before adding -ED, -ES, or -ING to *quiz*, ☐ double, ☐ do not double, final Z.　　　(double)

Chapter **13.**
HOW ETYMOLOGY EXPLAINS
SINGLE CONSONANTS

It's nice to have the kind of reliable rules that tell us when to double a final consonant, and when to leave it alone.

But Christmas doesn't come every day, especially in spelling.

Which is to say that the holiday is over as far as today's words are concerned—whether we use a single or a double consonant cannot be figured out according to any logical system, but will depend, for the most part, on each word's *etymology*—that is, on the spelling of the root from which the word is derived.

Although we will have no satisfactory broad principles to tie our words together, there will nevertheless be little difficulty in remembering whether to use a single or a double consonant—for by tracing and understanding the derivation of each spelling demon, we will be able to form a clear intellectual and visual response to it.

Notice, now, how easily and prettily this can be accomplished.

Words for Today

1. INOCULATE
   From Latin *oculus,* eye, and *in,* into—an eye, or bud, is made in the skin, into which the serum is injected. OCULIST, eye doctor, and OCULAR, pertaining to the eye, derive from the same root. Note, then, the single N *(in)* and single C *(oculus)*. Stare at the word for a moment, then write it in the blank:

   ....

2. RECOMMEND

From COMMEND, which logically has one C and two M's, plus the prefix *re-*, again. Become visually familiar with the one C, double M pattern.

Write the word: ....

3. VACUUM

From Latin *vacuus*, empty, used also in such English words as VACANT, VACATE, EVACUATE, all of which contain only one C. (To remember the double U, no great stumbling block for most people, get into the habit of pronouncing the word in three syllables: VAC-U-UM.)

Write the word: ....

4. VACUOUS

From the same root as VACUUM, it means figuratively empty, as a VACUOUS mind, stare, personality, etc. Resist the normal temptation to double the C.

Write the word: ....

5. EXHILARATE

From the Latin *hilaris*, glad, cheerful. This root is found also in HILARIOUS, which everyone spells correctly. Compare the two words, noting that both contain HILAR—one L, followed by A.

Write the word: ....

6. VILIFY

From the same Latin root which gives us VILE—hence one L. To VILIFY someone is to call him *vile*—that is, to describe him in slanderous, abusive, or defamatory language.

Write the word: ....

7. ACCELERATE

From Latin *celer*, fast, which also gives us the English words CELERITY, quickness, speed, and ACCEL-

ERATOR, the pedal which speeds up an automobile engine. Note the single L.

Write the word: ....

8. A<u>N</u>OINT
From the same Latin root from which the word *ointment* derives—to ANOINT is to rub with *an oil* or *an oint*ment, hence only one N following the A.

Write the word: ....

9. MILLIO<u>N</u>AIRE
From the word *million* plus the prefix *-aire*. BILLION-AIRE is constructed similarly, so both words have only one N. (Contradictorily, as we shall learn in a later chapter, *questionnaire* has two N's.)

Write the word: ....

10. I<u>R</u>IDESCENT
From *Iris,* Greek goddess of the rainbow. The IRIS of the eye and the girl's name (IRIS) come from the same source—and, as you notice, all of them have one R, followed by I. I<u>R</u>IDESCENT is almost universally misspelled (*irridescent, irredescent,* etc.), even by the most erudite.

Write the word: ....

11, 12. SHE<u>RIFF</u>, TA<u>RIFF</u>
These words are most efficiently learned together—note that each has one R, two F's. SHE<u>RIFF</u> was the officer, originally, of a *shire* in England, a territorial division now called a county—hence the single R.

TA<u>RIFF</u> comes from an Italian word *tariffa,* information or explanation—hence, again, the one R, two F's.

Write the words: ....

....

13. **CARESS**
This could just as logically have two R's, but the ultimate derivation is Latin *carus*, dear, beloved—hence only one R.

Write the word: ....

14. **HOLIDAY**
Originally *holy day*, hence one **L**.

Write the word: ....

15. **PROFESSOR**
A problem to some people who have an almost irresistible urge to use a double F, even though they have no trouble with the verb PROFESS, to which, of course, PROFESSOR is etymologically related.

Write the word: ....

16. **OCCASIONAL**
This word will surprise you in one of two ways—either that it appears here at all since you cannot imagine anyone's misspelling it; or that it has only one S, since you always write it with two. If you're surprised for the second reason, you belong to a vast group of people who quite naturally—but unthinkingly—double the S. But consider: TREASURE, MEASURE, LEISURE, all with the same ZH sound closing the first syllable, have only one S—OCCASIONAL, with an identical pronunciation of the S, provides no basis for doubling the consonant. The word derives from Latin *occasio*, a fit time.

Write the word: ....

17. **DESICCATED**
From Latin *siccus*, dry—hence, the surprising single S, double C, not the other way around. A word much used today by writers (means completely dried up, either literally or figuratively), and almost invariably misspelled.

Write the word: ....

Let's Practice

Today's 17 words are all characterized by a single consonant where logic or pronunciation might tempt the unwary
into incorrect doubling. Pointing out the exact place where
an error is usually made alerts the student and insures
against misspelling. But let's be doubly sure on single consonants. If I give you the meaning of each of these words,
plus its initial letter, can you make sure to avoid the
popular pitfall?

To inject (a person) against disease

(I-) ....   (INOCULATE)

Suggest favorably

(R-) ....   (RECOMMEND)

Empty space

(V-) ....   (VACUUM)

Figuratively empty

(V-) ....   (VACUOUS)

To enliven; cheer up and invigorate

(E-) ....   (EXHILARATE)

Spread malicious slander about

(V-) ....   (VILIFY)

Speed up

(A-) ....   (ACCELERATE)

Rub with oil

(A-) ....   (ANOINT)

Very rich person

(M-) ....   (MILLIO_N_AIRE)

Exhibiting a rainbowlike display
of color

(I-) ....   (IR_IDESCENT)

County peace officer

(S-) ....   (SHER_IF_F)

Tax on imports

(T-) ....   (TAR_IFF_)

Fondle lovingly

(C-) ....   (CAR_E_SS)

Religious festival; day of leisure

(H-) ....   (HOL_I_DAY)

College teacher

(P-) ....   (PROF_E_SSOR)

Happening at odd or irregular
intervals

(O-) ....   (OCCAS_I_ONAL)

Dried up

(D-) ....   (DESIC_C_ATED)

More Practice

Now you've written each word twice, concentrating particularly on the crucial areas. Try them once more, and it
will be impossible for you ever to misspell a single one. I'll
provide you with the beginnings and ends; you fill in the
missing letter or letters, then rewrite the complete word.

INO_ULATE

....   (INOCULATE)

RE___MEND

....   (RECOMMEND)

VA_UUM

....   (VACUUM)

EXHI_RATE

....   (EXHILARATE)

VL_IFY

....   (VILIFY)

ACCE_ERATE

....   (ACCELERATE)

A_OINT

....   (ANOINT)

MILLIO_AIRE

....   (MILLIONAIRE)

IR_DESCENT

....   (IRIDESCENT)

SH_IFF

....   (SHERIFF)

TA_IFF

....   (TARIFF)

CA_ESS

....   (CARESS)

HO_IDAY

....   (HOLIDAY)

PRO_ESSOR

....   (PROFESSOR)

OCCA_IONAL

....   (OCCASIONAL)

DES___ATED

....   (DESICCATED)

VA_UOUS

....   (VACUOUS)

A Thought for Tomorrow

Now that you've got the 17 most frequently misspelled single-consonant words under control, do you want to try a challenging list of pesky double-consonant words? That's our program in chapter 14.

Chapter 14.

DOUBLE CONSONANTS THAT ARE TRICKY

As we have said, a double consonant has, unfortunately, the same sound as a single consonant. Pronouncing a word carefully—except in isolated instances—is of no help in spelling it properly.

What does help is forming so strong a visual image of the correct pattern of a word that writing it any other way will do intolerable violence to your memory of it.

Strong, ineradicable visual images of correct patterns are achieved by concentrating on the slippery, usually misspelled part of a demon, and then writing the proper form as a response to meaningful situations.

So today you will continue training your visual memory by intelligent practice. I shall challenge you to associate certain words with double consonants—indeed, to develop so strong an association that immediately you hear, think of, or see any of the following words you will reflexively react with, "Ha! a double S"—or a double C, R, P, N, or whatever crucial letter is involved.

Words for Today

Let us start with S's. Note in the following that S appears only as a double consonant—and that, furthermore, no other consonant is doubled in any of the words. Look searchingly at each word with these points in mind, then cover it and rewrite.

ASSASSIN ....

COLOSSAL ....

DISSIPATE   ....

FRICASSEE   ....

HARASS   ....

NECESSARY   ....

ASSESS   ....

POSSESS   ....

Random Notes That Will Help You

Let's talk about some of these words a bit so that we can nail home the double S's.

In the 11th and 12th centuries there was a secret Mohammedan sect in the East called *Hashashin*, or hashish-eaters. Members chewed on hashish, a powerful opium-like drug made from hemp, to work themselves into a murderous frenzy before setting out to exterminate their enemies. It is from the Arabic *Hashashin* that our word ASSASSIN derives, and the twin sets of SH's account for the double S's. Related forms have corresponding patterns—ASSASSINATE, ASSASSINATION, etc.

One of the seven wonders of the ancient world was the *Colossus*, a 105-foot statue of Apollo, at the entrance to the harbor of Rhodes. It is from this word, with its single L and double S, that our adjective COLOSSAL derives—to describe anything gigantic, immense, or, as a Hollywood term, vulgarly spectacular.

One way to DISSIPATE, let us pretend, is to *sip Scotch* —the two S's, one P, and the important vowel I are all highlighted in this phrase.

FRICASSEE, a delightful stew of small pieces of meat, may be served at the table in a CASSEROLE—note the single C and double S in both words.

HARASS may be pronounced with the accent either on the first syllable (somewhat more sophisticated), or, more commonly, on the second. But only the S is doubled.

ASSESS and POSSESS have double consonants, and the only double consonant in either word is an S; and these twin sets are found in all derived forms of both words: ASSESSOR, ASSESSMENT, POSSESSOR, POSSESSION, PREPOSSESSING, REPOSSESS.

More Practice

Study these eight words once again, noting especially, this time, the underlined letters. Then cover each word and rewrite it.

ASSASSIN	....
COLOSSAL	....
DISSIPATE	....
FRICASSEE	....
HARASS	....
NECESSARY	....
ASSESS	....
POSSESS	....

And Still More

Now write the word that fits each definition and that starts with the letter indicated.

Have or hold

(P-) ....   (POSSESS)

Murderer

(A-) ....   (ASSASSIN)

Put a value on

(A-) ....   (A<u>SSE</u>SS)

Gigantic

(C-) ....   (COLO<u>SS</u>AL)

Essential

(N-) ....   (NEC<u>ESS</u>ARY)

Waste; live riotously

(D-) ....   (DI<u>SSI</u>PATE)

Persecute or annoy continually

(H-) ....   (HA<u>RASS</u>)

Meat stew

(F-) ....   (FRI<u>CASSE</u>E)

So much for double S. Let us concentrate now on words
in which a double N or double T will be crucial.

1. <u>INN</u>OCUOUS. Anything or anyone utterly harmless,
   unable to cause damage, hurt, or injury may be labeled
   <u>INN</u>OCUOUS. This word is built on the Latin root
   noc-, to injure, plus the negative prefix *in-;* hence the
   double N. Note that *innocent,* constructed similarly,
   also has two N's and one C.

   Write the word: ....

2. <u>INN</u>UENDO. Any indirect, and derogatory, remark,
   any sly and belittling allusion or hint, is an <u>INN</u>U-
   ENDO, <u>INN</u>UENDOES are generally not <u>INN</u>OCU-
   OUS, but both words start with a double N.

   Write the word: ....

3. QUESTIO<u>NN</u>AIRE. *Question* has one N, of course,
   as does every one of its derivatives (*questioning,*

questioner, etc.) with one glaring exception: QUES-TIONNAIRE—an especially odd spelling, since *millionaire, billionaire, concessionaire,* and similar formations have a single N. However, odd spellings are the easiest to remember.

Write the word: ....

4. TYRANNY. No one misspells *tyrant;* when it comes to others forms of this word, however, most spellers feel that some consonant needs doubling, but they're not quite sure whether it's the R or the N. It's the N. Hence, we write TYRANNY, TYRANNICAL, TYRANNOUS, TYRANNIZE. (Note that three of these are accented on the first syllable, one on the second—but all have two N's.) For the moment, concentrate on TYRANNY.

Write the word: ....

5. BATTALION. *Battle,* as everyone knows, has two T's, one L. (What else could it be?) A group of soldiers arrayed for *battle* has a similar pattern: BATTALION. The pronunciation might tempt some unwary spellers into doubling the L, as we do in *medallion,* but an awareness of the derivation of the word will reinforce the correct pattern in your mind.

Write the word: ....

6. DILETTANTE. One who dabbles in one of the fine arts is called a DILETTANTE—a double L suits the pronunciation better, but the origin of the word is the Italian *dilettare,* to delight, hence the double T.

Write the word: ....

7. STILETTO. Italian is also the language from which we get STILETTO, literally a little dagger—and again, as in *dilettante,* we use a single L, a double T.

Write the word: ....

8. MULATTO. The same pattern of one L and two T's is found in MULATTO, though this word comes from the Portuguese.

Write the word: ....

9. GUTTURAL. The Latin word for throat, *guttur*, is responsible for English GUTTURAL—and just as crucial as the double T is the U following it.

Write the word: ....

10. SPAGHETTI. For our last word we go back to Italian, a language with a fondness for double T's. In SPA-GHETTI, which etymologically means *small cords*, we also want to watch that H after the G.

Write the word: ....

Let's Practice

You will be amazed at how permanently the correct spelling of a word will lodge in your mind once you learn to concentrate on the one or two crucial areas in which errors most frequently occur. Pay particular attention, now, to the underlined letters in each word, then cover the word and write it once again.

INNOCUOUS   ....

INNUENDO   ....

QUESTIONNAIRE   ....

TYRANNY   ....

BATTALION   ....

DILETTANTE   ....

STILETTO   ....

MULATTO   ....

GUTTURAL   ....

SPAGHETTI   ....

These ten words, together with the first eight in this chapter are among the most frequently misspelled in the language. Each contains either a double S, a double N, or a double T—and, you have noticed, *no other consonant in the word is doubled*. With this principle in mind, fill in the missing consonants in the following, then rewrite each word.

1. A__A__IN   .... (SS, SS)

2. CO_O__AL   .... (L, SS)

3. DI__LATE   .... (SS, P)

4. FRI_A__EE   .... (C, SS)

5. HA_A__   .... (R, SS)

6. NECE__ARY   .... (SS)

7. A__ESS   .... (SS)

8. PO__ESS   .... (SS)

9. I_O_UOUS   .... (NN, C)

10. I__UENDO   .... (NN)

11. QUESTIO__AIRE   .... (NN)

12. TY_A__Y   .... (R, NN)

13. BA__A_ION   .... (TT, L)

14. DI_E__ANTE   .... (L, TT)

15. STI_E__O   .... (L, TT)

16. MU_A__O   .... (L, TT)

17. GU__URAL   .... (TT)

18. SPAGHE__I   .... (TT)

How well do you transfer your learning to other words?

Below are various forms of some of the 18 words we have studied. Can you fill in the missing letters correctly, and then rewrite the word?

1. A_A_INATION .... (SS, SS)

2. DI_LATION .... (SS, P)

3. HA_A_MENT .... (R, SS)

4. NECE_ITY .... (SS)

5. A_ESSMENT .... (SS)

6. PO_ESSION .... (SS)

7. PREPO_ESSING .... (SS)

8. TY_A_ICAL .... (R, NN)

9. TY_A_OUS .... (R, NN)

10. TY_A_IZE .... (R, NN)

Other letters, besides the double consonants, are sometimes error-producing in a number of these words. If you have been training your visual memory properly, you should be able to fill in the missing parts.

1. DISS_PATE .... (I)

2. FRICASS_ .... (EE)

3. NECESS_RY .... (A)

4. M_LATTO .... (U)

5. GUTT_RAL .... (U)

6. SPA_ETTI .... (GH)

A Thought for Tomorrow

Have you been working so well on chapters 9 through 14 that you are prepared for a full-dress examination of your spelling skill? And what if I slip in a number of words from chapters 2 to 7? In the next chapter, you will be challenged to make a perfect score on a representative sampling of all past words.

Chapter 15.

SECOND REVIEW TEST

I. Of the following 20 words, some are spelled correctly, others are deliberately misspelled. If the pattern looks right to you, check the blank. If you detect an error, re-write the word.

1. oscillate .... (√)
2. tittilate .... (titillate)
3. vaccilate .... (vacillate)
4. flagellate .... (√)
5. scintilate .... (scintillate)
6. allotment .... (√)
7. colaborate .... (collaborate)
8. paralell .... (parallel)
9. sattelite .... (satellite)
10. miscellaneous .... (√)
11. alright .... (all right)
12. baloon .... (balloon)
13. ellipse .... (√)
14. tonsilitis .... (tonsillitis)
15. villain .... (√)
16. skillful .... (√)
17. wholly .... (√)

18. mettalic   .... (metallic)

19. occurence   .... (occurrence)

20. annullment   .... (annulment)

II. Find the *one* misspelled word on each line and rewrite it correctly.

1. reference, preference, conference,
   recurence.

   ....   (recurrence)

2. annulled, controlled, revelled,
   expelled.

   ....   (reveled)

3. committed, acquitted, allotted,
   benefitted.

   ....   (benefited)

4. traveled, worshiped, equiped,
   walloped.

   ....   (equipped)

5. kidnaped, banqueted, quized,
   libeled.

   ....   (quizzed)

III. Every word in the following list contains a common error. Can you find it, and then rewrite the word correctly?

1. inocculate   .... (inoculate)

2. reccomend   .... (recommend)

3. vaccum   .... (vacuum)

4. vaccuous   .... (vacuous)

5. exhillerate .... (exhilarate)

6. villify .... (vilify)

7. accellerate .... (accelerate)

8. annoint .... (anoint)

9. millionnaire .... (millionaire)

10. irredescent .... (iridescent)

11. sherrif .... (sheriff)

12. carress .... (caress)

13. holliday .... (holiday)

14. proffesor .... (professor)

15. occassional .... (occasional)

16. dessicated .... (desiccated)

IV. Can you unerringly choose the correct form when two or more spellings are offered you?

1. (a) tariff, (b) tarrif	(a)
2. (a) asassin, (b) assassin	(b)
3. (a) collosal, (b) colossal	(b)
4. (a) dissapate, (b) dissipate, (c) disippate	(b)
5. (a) fricassee, (b) friccasee, (c) fricasse	(a)
6. (a) asess, (b) assess	(b)
7. (a) posess, (b) possess	(b)
8. (a) inoccuous, (b) innocuous	(b)
9. (a) inuendo, (b) innuendo	(b)
10. (a) questionnaire, (b) questionaire	(a)
11. (a) tyrrany, (b) tyranny	(b)
12. (a) battalion, (b) batallion	(a)
13. (a) dilettante, (b) dilletante	(a)
14. (a) stilleto, (b) stiletto	(b)
15. (a) mullato, (b) mulatto	(b)
16. (a) gutteral, (b) guttural	(b)

17. (a) spaghetti, (b) spagetti   (a)
18. (a) tyrannize, (b) tyrranize   (a)

V. Decide whether each of the following words ends in
-IZE or -ISE, and add the correct suffix.

1. verbal..........   (ize)

2. desp..........   (ise)

3. advert..........   (ise)

4. local..........   (ize)

5. surm..........   (ise)

6. galvan..........   (ize)

7. superv..........   (ise)

8. surpr..........   (ise)

9. organ..........   (ize)

10. chast..........   (ise)

VI. On each line *one* word is misspelled. Find it and rewrite it correctly.

1. newsstand, bookkeeper, suddeness,
   drunkenness.

   ....   (suddenness)

2. sincerely, lonely, solely, embarassment.

   ....   (embarrassment)

3. dissapear, misspelling, misshapen,
   dissatisfy.

   ....   (disappear)

4. coolly, incidently, accidentally, really.

   ....   (incidentally)

5. equipment, development, harassment, envelopement.

   .... (envelopment)

6. recieve, believe, achieve, niece.

   .... (receive)

7. weird, leisure, seize, seige.

   .... (siege)

8. hygeine, Hygeia, Sheila, inveigle.

   .... (hygiene)

9. counterfeit, foreign, heifer, seive.

   .... (sieve)

Chapter 16.

-ANCE AND -ENCE (I)

It is because so many similar or even identical sounds are represented by different letters that English is the most difficult of modern languages to spell correctly.

RESISTANCE, for example, ends in -ANCE, PERSISTENCE in -ENCE; but the suffixes are pronounced exactly the same way.

The noun DESCENDANT terminates in -ANT (though the infrequently used adjective is preferably spelled -ENT); the noun SUPERINTENDENT has an -ENT ending.

There is, unfortunately, no rule to guide you when faced with a choice between -ANCE and -ENCE, or the related -ANT and -ENT. The use of A or E is determined by something as abstruse as the type of Latin verb from which each word is derived, so it would seem that only a scholar of classical languages could ever be sure.

Oddly enough, most people nevertheless make proper choices *most of the time,* relying, without giving it a second thought, on visual memory they have built up over years of seeing -ANCE, -ENCE words in print.

Yes, generally, the hundreds of words that end one way or the other cause little confusion—*except for some 30 special demons that either look good both ways or that perversely have a greater appeal with the incorrect suffix than with the correct one.*

These demons will be our sole concern today—you will have a chance to master them so completely, to commit them so strongly to visual memory, that error and confusion will vanish.

Words for Today

We start with the 16 most frequently misspelled -ENCE, -ENT words. Examine each one carefully, concentrating first on the suffix, then on the whole word, reacting to it visually in such a way that an A in either ending will henceforth look tortured and deformed to you.

SUPERINTENDENCE	....
SUPERINTENDENT	....
DEPENDENCE	....
DEPENDENT	....
PERSISTENCE	....
PERSISTENT	....
INSISTENCE	....
INSISTENT	....
INADVERTENCE	....
INADVERTENT	....
OPULENCE	....
OPULENT	....
EXISTENCE	....
EXISTENT	....
SUBSISTENCE	....
SUBSISTENT	....
SENTENCE	....
CONFIDENCE	....
CONFIDENT	....
DIFFIDENCE	....

DIFFIDENT   ....

DIFFERENCE   ....

DIFFERENT   ....

ANTECEDENCE   ....

ANTECEDENT   ....

PENITENCE   ....

PENITENT   ....

ABSTINENCE   ....

ABSTINENT   ....

INTERMITTENCE   ....

INTERMITTENT   ....

Let's Practice

You've made a start at being comfortable with the -ENCE or -ENT ending in the 16 words. Let's aim now to make assurance doubly sure by writing these words a number of times as meaningful responses in the following exercises.

I. Add -ENT to each root, then write a brief phrase using the word.

SUPERINTEND___

....

DEPEND___

....

PERSIST___

....

INSIST____

....

INADVERT____

....

OPUL____

....

EXIST____

....

SUBSIST____

....

CONFID____

....

DIFFID____

....

DIFFER____

....

ANTECED____

....

PENIT____

....

ABSTIN____

....

INTERMITT____

....

II. Write the word, ending in -ENCE, that fits each definition. Initial letters are provided to jog your thinking.

1. Act of abstaining, especially from food, liquor, and other bodily pleasures

    (AB-)   .... (ABSTINENCE)

2. State of being

    (EX-)   .... (EXISTENCE)

3. Absentmindedness; lack of attention

    (IN-)   .... (INADVERTENCE)

4. Assurance; belief; faith

    (CON-)   .... (CONFIDENCE)

5. Management; control

    (SU-)   .... (SUPERINTENDENCE)

6. Dissimilarity

    (DIF-)   .... (DIFFERENCE)

7. Subordination; reliance

    (DEP-)   .... (DEPENDENCE)

8. Lack of confidence; shyness

    (DIF-)   .... (DIFFIDENCE)

9. Stubbornness; continuation

    (PER-)   .... (PERSISTENCE)

10. Great wealth or luxury

    (OP-)   .... (OPULENCE)

11. Demandingness

    (INS-)   .... (INSISTENCE)

12. Group of words forming a complete

    thought

    (SEN-)   .... (SENTENCE)

13. Means of support

    (SUB-)   .... (SUBSISTENCE)

14. Sorrow for wrongdoing

    (PEN-)   .... (PENITENCE)

15. Act or quality of preceding

    (ANT-)   .... (ANTECEDENCE)

16. Discontinuity; state or act of

    occurring at interrupted intervals

    (INTER-)   .... (INTERMITTENCE)

More Words for Today

You will recall from chapter 11 that certain verbs ending
in -R preceded by a single vowel were accented on the final
syllable (*occur, deter, abhor,* etc.), and that the accent in
a number of them remained on that syllable when a suffix
was added (*occurred, deterring,* etc.). Six of these are occasionally misspelled with the improper noun ending. Note the
following, and rewrite the noun form.

VERB	ENDING	NOUN	
OCCUR	(-ENCE)	....	(OCCURRENCE)

RECUR   (-ENCE) ....(RECURRENCE)

INCUR   (-ENCE) ....(INCURRENCE)

CONCUR   (-ENCE) ....(CONCURRENCE)

DETER   (-ENCE) ....(DETERRENCE)

ABHOR   (-ENCE) ....(ABHORRENCE)

Adjective forms will, of course, end in -ENT.

RECURRENT   ....

CONCURRENT   ....

DETERRENT   ....

ABHORRENT   ....

Let's Practice

I. Which noun fits each definition?

1. Loathing

   (AB-)   ....   (ABHORRENCE)

2. Happening

   (OC-)   ....   (OCCURRENCE)

3. A stopping of someone from
   doing something

   (DE-)   ....   (DETERRENCE)

4. Repetition of a happening

   (RE-)   ....   (RECURRENCE)

5. A happening together; agreement

   (CON-)   ....   (CONCURRENCE)

6. A bringing (of something unpleasant) upon oneself

   (IN-) .... (INCURRENCE)

II. Write the noun form of each of these verbs.

1. INCUR

   .... (INCURRENCE)

2. CONCUR

   .... (CONCURRENCE)

3. ABHOR

   .... (ABHORRENCE)

4. DETER

   .... (DETERRENCE)

5. RECUR

   .... (RECURRENCE)

6. OCCUR

   .... (OCCURRENCE)

A Thought for Tomorrow

For most people, no more than 22 words ending in -ENCE cause any confusion. Add to these ten words ending in -ANCE that are often misspelled, and you have a total of 32 words which, once conquered, will remove all your -ANCE, -ENCE difficulties.

The ten important -ANCE demons will occupy our attention in the next chapter.

Chapter 17.

-ANCE AND -ENCE (II)

So now we have the 22 -ENCE demons under control. Ready to try your hand at the -ANCE group?

Words for Today

Study each word carefully, concentrating particularly on the ending; then cover and rewrite.

RESIST_ANCE_ ....

RELEV_ANCE_ ....

PERSEVER_ANCE_ ....

REPENT_ANCE_ ....

ATTEND_ANCE_ ....

MAINTEN_ANCE_ ....

SUSTEN_ANCE_ ....

PETUL_ANCE_ ....

APPEAR_ANCE_ ....

ABUND_ANCE_ ....

(Not many -ANCE words bedevil the average speller. Conquer these ten and the likelihood of being tempted to write -ENCE where -ANCE is required is small.)

Other forms of these words will, of course, end in -ANT, not -ENT. Practice these.

RESIST*ANT*   ....

RELEV*ANT*   ....

REPENT*ANT*   ....

ATTEND*ANT*   ....

PETUL*ANT*   ....

ABUND*ANT*   ....

The noun DESCENDANT troubles many people. Consider that a DESCEND*ANT* comes from an *AN*CESTOR, and you'll have this demon under complete control. (The infrequently used adjective, as I have said, is spelled *descendent*—but don't worry about it.)

Negatives follow the pattern of the affirmative forms: *unresistant, irrelevant, unrepentant,* etc.

Be especially wary of PERSEVERANCE—many writers tend to put an unnecessary R before the V. Think of SEVERE, add PER-, then clip the final E and attach -ANCE: PERSEVERANCE.

And watch RELEVANT too—note that the L precedes the V, not the other way around, as also in IRRELEVANT, and in the corresponding noun forms, RELEVANCE and IRRELEVANCE.

A little extra care, too, on MAINTENANCE and SUSTENANCE. Though the verbs are MAINTAIN and SUSTAIN, the middle syllable of the nouns are nevertheless -TEN-: MAINTENANCE, SUSTENANCE.

Let's Practice

You've come to terms, now, with ten -ANCE nouns and one special -ANT form (DESCENDANT). Nail mastery down permanently, now, by adding the required ending to each root, then rewriting the complete word.

I. Add -ANCE.

abund........   relev........

....

mainten........   persever........

....

attend........   appear........

....

resist........   susten........

....

repent........   petul........

....

II. Add -ANT.

abund........   repent........

....

attend........   relev........

....

resist........   petul........

....

descend........   unrepent........

....

unresist........   irrelev........

....

Chapter 18.

RUNDOWN ON -ANCE, -ENCE

Of all the -ANCE, -ENCE; -ANT, -ENT words, only the 33 we have worked with in preceding chapters cause any real perplexity to the average speller. The odds are overwhelming that if the proper endings for these less than three dozen demons are a vital, integral part of your visual and muscular memory, you'll rarely, if ever, fall prey to error on any words containing one or the other ending. So glance once again over chapters 16 and 17, and then see how close to a perfect score you can come in the following review exercises.

I. Finish each word with the correct ending, -ANT or -ENT.

superintend........	(ent)	repent........	(ant)
resist........	(ant)	depend........	(ent)
penit........	(ent)	persist........	(ent)
inadvert........	(ent)	insist........	(ent)
relev........	(ant)	anteced........	(ent)
attend........	(ant)	differ........	(ent)
opul........	(ent)	diffid........	(ent)
confid........	(ent)	irrelev........	(ant)
petul........	(ant)	descend........	(ant)
abund........	(ant)	intermitt........	(ent)
abstin........	(ent)		

II. Change the following verbs into nouns.

abhor	.... (abhorrence)
deter	.... (deterrence)
occur	.... (occurrence)
recur	.... (recurrence)
incur	.... (incurrence)
concur	.... (concurrence)

III. Add either -ANCE or -ENCE, whichever is correct.

persever........	(ance)	susten........	(ance)
exist........	(ence)	depend........	(ence)
subsist........	(ence)	resist........	(ance)
mainten........	(ance)	persist........	(ence)
sent........	(ence)	insist........	(ence)

Chapter 19.

DANGEROUS VOWELS

If only words were spelled in English the way they're pronounced (as they are, fairly consistently, in French, Spanish, Italian, and many other languages), we would have no insecure spellers, no educated people unable to turn out a page of writing without errors.

But, as I have pointed out so often, the same sound is represented in any number of different ways in our language, and only the person who has repeatedly trained his visual and muscular memory can feel sure that he avoids mistakes.

Take, for today, the problem of the "obscure vowel." An obscure vowel occurs in a syllable that does not receive the accent in pronunciation—for example, the A in *sofa,* the first E in *believe,* the first I in *discrimination,* the O in *collaborate,* or the second U in *guttural.* With a little thought, you will readily see that all five of these vowels have identical pronunciations in the particular words offered—a quick sound and nothing more. (Unlike, by contrast, the A in *wastrel,* the E in *setting,* the I in *pillow,* the O in *polar,* or the U in *mugger.*)

So the problem often arises (not too often, fortunately—only in certain confusing and frequently misspelled words), how do we spell this obscure vowel—with an A, an E, an I, an O, or a U? (In syllables with accented vowels, on the contrary, there is almost never any room for doubt.)

Words for Today

Let's start with six problem words in which the obscure vowel sound is represented by A, though it could be just as logically indicated by any of the other four vowels. Consider each of the following, concentrating particularly on the underlined vowel, then rewrite the complete word.

1. SEP<u>A</u>RATE   ....

2. COMPAR<u>A</u>TIVE   ....

3. V<u>A</u>NILLA   ....

4. DEM<u>A</u>GOGUE   ....

5. PED<u>A</u>GOGUE   ....

6. SYN<u>A</u>GOGUE   ....

Now, note the following 12 demons in which the letter E represents the obscure vowel sound.

7. D<u>E</u>SPAIR   ....

8. DESP<u>E</u>RATE   ....

9. D<u>E</u>SCRIBE   ....

10. D<u>E</u>SCRIPTION   ....

11. IND<u>E</u>SCRIBABLE   ....

12. D<u>E</u>VISE   ....

13. CAT<u>E</u>GORY   ....

14. MATH<u>E</u>MATICS   ....

15. PHENOM<u>E</u>NAL   ....

16. PHENOM<u>E</u>NON   ....

17. SIN<u>E</u>CURE   ....

18. VIN<u>E</u>GAR   ....

In the following, the obscure vowel sound is indicated by the letter I.

19. D<u>I</u>VIDE   ....

20. DISCRIMINATE   ....
21. RIDICULOUS   ....
22. DEFINITELY   ....
23. ELIGIBLE   ....
24. COMPARISON   ....
25. SENSITIVE   ....

In our 26th word, RHINOCEROS, the final O is important; in words 27 and 28, PURSUIT and GUTTURAL, the underlined U is often a problem.

Write these three words:

26. RHINOCEROS   ....
27. PURSUIT   ....
28. GUTTURAL   ....

Let's Practice

These 28 words are often misspelled; and the point of error is the vowel sound that can logically be represented by any one of the five vowels. So, for added practice, first fill in the missing vowel, then rewrite the complete word.

PHENOM_NON   .... (E)
COMPAR_TIVE   .... (A)
COMPAR_SON   .... (I)
DESP_RATE   .... (E)
D_SPAIR   .... (E)
D_SCRIBE   .... (E)
D_VIDE   .... (I)
D_SCRIMINATE   .... (I)

D_VISE .... (E)

R_DICULOUS .... (I)

V_NILLA .... (A)

CAT_GORY .... (E)

DEM_GOGUE .... (A)

P_RSUIT .... (U)

RHINOCER_S .... (O)

D_SCRIPTION .... (E)

DEFIN_TELY .... (I)

SENS_TIVE .... (I)

GUTT_RAL .... (U)

SIN_CURE .... (E)

PED_GOGUE .... (A)

MATH_MATICS .... (E)

EL_GIBLE .... (I)

VIN_GAR .... (E)

IND_SCRIBABLE .... (E)

SYN_GOGUE .... (A)

PHENOM_NAL .... (E)

SEP_RATE .... (A)

Chapter 21.
DROPPING FINAL E

So if a word ends in -CE or -GE, we *retain* final E before adding -ABLE.

Suppose a word ends in E preceded by some consonant *other than C or G*?

Then, we have decided, we drop E before adding -ABLE.

For example, PLEASURE becomes PLEASURABLE, LIVE becomes LIVABLE, DESIRE becomes DESIRABLE, EXCUSE becomes EXCUSABLE, DESCRIBE becomes DESCRIBABLE, and so on.

It is true that a few variant spellings are technically correct, for instance, LIKEABLE, LOVEABLE, SIZEABLE, etc.; but, though correct, these forms are rarely enough used for you to avoid them. Be safe, stay consistent, and always drop final E after any consonant but C or G when adding -ABLE.

Words for Today (I)

Again, I ask you to make your own word list. Change each of the following to an adjective by adding -ABLE, remembering to drop final E if the preceding letter is any consonant except C or G.

PLEASURE plus -ABLE

....   (PLEASURABLE)

DESIRE plus -ABLE

....   (DESIRABLE)

EXCUSE plus -ABLE

....   (EXCUSABLE)

DESCRIBE plus -ABLE

....   (DESCRIBABLE)

LIKE plus -ABLE

....   (LIKABLE)

LOVE plus -ABLE

....   (LOVABLE)

ENFORCE plus -ABLE

....   (ENFORCEABLE)

SIZE plus -ABLE

....   (SIZABLE)

USE plus -ABLE

....   (USABLE)

PROVE plus -ABLE

....   (PROVABLE)

MOVE plus -ABLE

....   (MOVABLE)

BLAME plus -ABLE

....   (BLAMABLE)

NOTICE plus -ABLE

....   (NOTICEABLE)

SALE plus -ABLE

....   (SALABLE)

VALUE plus -ABLE

....   (VALUABLE)

ARGUE plus -ABLE

....   (ARGUABLE)

MANAGE plus -ABLE

....   (MANAGEABLE)

DEPLORE plus -ABLE

....   (DEPLORABLE)

DEBATE plus -ABLE

....   (DEBATABLE)

PRESUME plus -ABLE

....   (PRESUMABLE)

CHANGE plus -ABLE

....   (CHANGEABLE)

HATE plus -ABLE

....   (HATABLE)

ADVISE plus -ABLE

....   (ADVISABLE)

ADMIRE plus -ABLE

....   (ADMIRABLE)

LIVE plus -ABLE

....   (LIVABLE)

Let's talk some more about dropping E's. The hallmark of the really poor speller is that he fails to drop an E that should be dropped, and, indeed, often goes so far as to insert an E in the unlikeliest places. *An inadequate speller is enamored of superfluous E's.*

If you are, too, let me see whether I cannot cool your ardor for this letter. Would you like to feel absolutely secure about when to use an E, when not to?

Recall, first, that we generally drop final E, preceded by any consonant except C or G, before adding -ABLE.

We can now go much further. We are going to drop final E, *no matter what consonant precedes it,* before any *other* suffix that starts with a vowel.

What are some suffixes, besides -ABLE, that start with vowels? The common ones that spring readily to mind are -ER, -OR, -ING, -ED, -AL, and -OUS. Thus, ADVISE becomes ADVISER; SUPERVISE becomes SUPERVISOR; NOTICE becomes NOTICING; MANAGE becomes MANAGED; ARRIVE becomes ARRIVAL; PORE becomes POROUS.

Easy enough so far? Then try your hand at adding the indicated suffix to each of the words in the following list.

Words for Today (II)

Write the word that results from the addition of the indicated suffix to each root.

ACHE plus -ING

....   (ACHING)

ADVISE plus -ING

....   (ADVISING)

COME plus -ING

....   (COMING)

HOPE plus -ING

....   (HOPING)

SEVERE plus -ITY

....   (SEVERITY)

DESIRE plus -OUS

....   (DESIROUS)

USE plus -ING

....   (USING)

CONFUSE plus -ION

....   (CONFUSION)

REVERSE plus -IBLE

....   (REVERSIBLE)

ARRIVE plus -AL

....   (ARRIVAL)

DESIRE plus -ING

....   (DESIRING)

PARE plus -ING

....   (PARING)

BELIEVE plus -ABLE

....   (BELIEVABLE)

ARGUE plus -ING

....   (ARGUING)

We generally consider that there are five vowels—A, E, I, O, U. But this is not entirely true. To begin with, U functions much more as a consonant after G or Q, as in ARGUE (where it has a Y sound), or in GUAVA and GUATEMALA (in which words it sounds like a W). And the letter Y, often a consonant in words like YES, YOU,

YEARN, YARD, etc., functions as a vowel when it sounds like an I, as in RHYTHM, GYMNASIUM, LONELY, CYST, etc.

As a suffix, Y is always considered a vowel. So, following the principle under which we are operating in this chapter, if we add the suffix -Y to words like STONE, BONE, SPONGE, or STAGE, we drop final E and get STONY, BONY, SPONGY, STAGY. (STAGEY is also correct, but it is preferable to drop the E.)

Let's Review Our Principles So Far

Let me repeat that memorizing rules in spelling is unnecessary. What is important is understanding and being able to apply the rules. So test your learning by completing the following statements.

1. Words ending in -CE and -GE retain final .... before -ABLE.   (E)

2. This is to keep the C or G
   "............" before the vowel A.   (soft)

3. Thus, NOTICE plus -ABLE is
   spelled ....   (NOTICEABLE)

4. And MANAGE plus -ABLE is
   spelled ....   (MANAGEABLE)

5. But in words ending in E
   preceded by any other con-
   sonant, final E is ....   (dropped)
   before -ABLE.

6. Thus, LOVE plus -ABLE is
   spelled ....   (LOVABLE)

7. If a word ends in E preceded by a consonant, final E is usually dropped before any suffix that starts with a .... (vowel)

8. Thus, COME plus -ING is spelled .... (COMING)

9. When -Y is a suffix, it is considered a .... (vowel)

10. Hence, final -E preceded by a consonant is .... be-fore adding the suffix -Y. (dropped)

11. Thus, SPONGE plus -Y is spelled .... (SPONGY)

12. And STONE plus -Y is spelled .... (STONY)

A Thought for Tomorrow

Now the question occurs to us, are there some special rules for *keeping* final E? There are, as we shall see in chapter 22.

Chapter 22.
ADDING SUFFIXES

We have decided that final E is generally dropped before a suffix that starts with a vowel, words like NOTICEABLE and CHANGEABLE being special, but logical, exceptions.

What if the suffix to be added starts with a consonant? For example, if we add -MENT to MANAGE, or -LY to LIKE?

Then, as you have probably already surmised, we *retain* final E.

Words for Today (I)

Shall we try a few? Add the indicated suffix to each word.

1. MERE plus -LY

.... (MER<u>E</u>LY)

2. LONE plus -LY

.... (LON<u>E</u>LY)

3. LONE plus -LINESS

.... (LON<u>E</u>LINESS)

4. SINCERE plus -LY

.... (SINCER<u>E</u>LY)

5. IMMEDIATE plus -LY

.... (IMMEDIAT<u>E</u>LY)

6. IMMENSE plus -LY

....   (IMMENS**E**LY)

7. RARE plus -LY

....   (RAR**E**LY)

8. BARE plus -LY

....   (BAR**E**LY)

9. DECISIVE plus -NESS

....   (DECISIV**E**NESS)

10. ADVERTISE plus -MENT

....   (ADVERTIS**E**MENT)

11. MEASURE plus -MENT

....   (MEASUR**E**MENT)

12. TRUE plus -NESS

....   (TRU**E**NESS)

What if -MENT is to be added to a word that does *not* end in E? This question may sound silly to you until I tell you that many poor spellers insert an E anyway! They will write *equipement* or *developement*, even though these words are composed of EQUIP plus -MENT, and DEVELOP plus -MENT. Are you sure this superfluous E never occurs in *your* spelling?

Words for Today (II)

Add -MENT to the following:

13. EQUIP

....   (EQUIP**M**ENT)

14. DEVELOP

....   (DEVELO<u>PM</u>ENT)

15. EMBARRASS

....   (EMBARRA<u>SS</u>ENT) (EMBARRAS<u>SM</u>ENT)

16. ENVELOP

....   (ENVELO<u>PM</u>ENT)

17. ABOLISH

....   (ABOLI<u>SHM</u>ENT)

18. ACCOMPLISH

....   (ACCOMPLI<u>SHM</u>ENT)

19. HARASS

....   (HARAS<u>SM</u>ENT)

So far, so good. Everything has gone according to rule, so there must be a catch somewhere. There is.

Certain important words, frequently misspelled, are exceptions to the rule we have been working with.

But exceptions, as you will soon realize, are easy to keep in mind precisely because they are exceptional. (We tend to remember what's different because of its conspicuousness.)

Consider, first, a group of words in which final E is preferably *dropped* before -MENT.

We have just said that final E is retained before -MENT, as in ENCOURAGEMENT, ADVERTISEMENT, and MEASUREMENT.

But if a word ends in -DGE, final E is perversely dropped in the preferable spelling.

Let's try some of these.

Words for Today (III)

Add -MENT to the following:

20. JUDGE

.... (JUDGMENT)

21. LODGE

.... (LODGMENT)

22. ABRIDGE

.... (ABRIDGMENT)

23. ACKNOWLEDGE

.... (ACKNOWLEDGMENT)

More exceptions. The final E of ARGUE should, by rule, be retained before -MENT. *It is dropped.* Correct form: ARGUMENT.

The final E of DUE, TRUE, ONE, and WHOLE should be retained before -LY. *It is dropped.* Correct forms: DULY, TRULY, ONLY, WHOLLY. (This final word may look peculiar to you—try to get used to it.)

The final E of HOLE should be dropped before the suffix -Y. *It is retained,* since HOLY means pious or religious, and we want a word meaning full of holes. Correct form: HOLEY.

And the final E of CAGE should also be dropped before -Y. In the preferable spelling *it is retained:* CAGEY. (CAGY is also correct, but not as common.)

The final E of AWE should be retained before -FUL. *It is dropped.* Correct form: AWFUL.

Finally, the final E of ACRE should be dropped before -AGE. *It is retained.* Correct form: ACREAGE (pronounced AY-ker-idge).

Words for Today (IV)

Practice, now, on the exceptions we have just discussed. Concentrate particularly on the underlined letter or letters, then rewrite each word.

24. AR**G**UMENT   ....

25. D**U**LY   ....

26. TR**U**LY   ....

27. O**N**LY   ....

28. ACR**E**AGE   ....

29. WHO**LL**Y   ....

30. HOL**E**Y   ....

31. CAG**E**Y   ....

32. A**W**FUL   ....

Let's Practice

Ready for a test on the 32 words in today's chapter? Every word below is either misspelled or spelled in its less preferable form. Cross it out, and rewrite it correctly.

1. merly

   ....   (MER**E**LY)

2. lonly

   ....   (LON**E**LY)

3. lonliness

   ....   (LON**E**LINESS)

4. sincerly

   ....   (SINCER**E**LY)

5. immensly

....   (IMMENS<u>E</u>LY)

6. rarly

....   (RAR<u>E</u>LY)

7. barly

....   (BAR<u>E</u>LY)

8. immediatly

....   (IMMEDIAT<u>E</u>LY)

9. decisivness

....   (DECISIV<u>E</u>NESS)

10. advertisment

....   (ADVERTIS<u>E</u>MENT)

11. measurment

....   (MEASUR<u>E</u>MENT)

12. truness

....   (TRU<u>E</u>NESS)

13. equipement

....   (EQUI<u>PM</u>ENT)

14. developement

....   (DEVELO<u>PM</u>ENT)

15. embarrassement

....   (EMBARRAS<u>SM</u>ENT)

16. envelopement

....   (ENVELO<u>PM</u>ENT)

17. abolishement

.... (ABOLI<u>SH</u>MENT)

18. accomplishement

.... (ACCOMPLI<u>SH</u>MENT)

19. harassement

.... (HARAS<u>SM</u>ENT)

20. judgement

.... (JU<u>DG</u>MENT)

21. lodgement

.... (LO<u>DG</u>MENT)

22. abridgement

.... (ABRI<u>DG</u>MENT)

23. acknowledgement

.... (ACKNOWLE<u>DG</u>MENT)

24. arguement

.... (ARGU<u>M</u>ENT)

25. duely

.... (D<u>UL</u>Y)

26. truely

.... (TR<u>UL</u>Y)

27. onely

.... (O<u>NL</u>Y)

28. wholely

.... (WHO<u>LL</u>Y)

29. holy *(full of holes)*

.... (HOL<u>E</u>Y)

30. cagy

.... (CAG<u>E</u>Y)

31. aweful

.... (A<u>W</u>FUL)

32. acrage

.... (ACR<u>E</u>AGE)

Chapter 23.

THIRD REVIEW TEST

I. Complete each word with either -ANT or -ENT, according to which suffix is required by the correct spelling, then rewrite.

1. superintend........   .... (ent)

2. depend........   .... (ent)

3. resist........   .... (ant)

4. inadvert........   .... (ent)

5. persist........   .... (ent)

6. insist........   .... (ent)

7. relev........   .... (ant)

8. opul........   .... (ent)

9. repent........   .... (ant)

10. diffid........   .... (ent)

11. abund........   .... (ant)

12. intermitt........   .... (ent)

13. attend........   .... (ant)

14. confid........   .... (ent)

15. anteced........   .... (ent)

16. abstin........   .... (ent)

II. Complete each word with either -ANCE or -ENCE, according to which suffix is required by the correct spelling, then rewrite.

1. exist........ .... (ence)

2. subsist........ .... (ence)

3. sent........ .... (ence)

4. persever........ .... (ance)

5. mainten........ .... (ance)

6. susten........ .... (ance)

7. occurr........ .... (ence)

8. recurr........ .... (ence)

9. irrelev........ .... (ance)

10. attend........ .... (ance)

11. concurr........ .... (ence)

12. deterr........ .... (ence)

13. abhorr........ .... (ence)

14. exist........ .... (ence)

15. subsist........ .... (ence)

16. appear........ .... (ance)

III. Fill in the missing letter or letters, then rewrite.

1. occu........nce .... (rre)

2. recu........nce .... (rre)

3. incu........nce .... (rre)

4. dete........nce .... (rre)

5. abho........nce .... (rre)

6. concu.......nce .... (rre)

7. perse....erance .... (v)

8. maint....nance .... (e)

9. sust....nance .... (e)

10. irre........vance .... (le)

11. sep....rate .... (a)

12. p....rsuit .... (u)

13. phenom... nal .... (e)

14. dem....gogue .... (a)

15. cat....gory .... (e)

16. vin....gar .... (e)

17. v....nilla .... (a)

18. r....diculous .... (i)

19. el....gible .... (i)

20. d....vise .... (e)

21. d....vide .... (i)

22. d....scribe .... (e)

23. d....scriminate .... (i)

24. d....spair .... (e)

25. el....gible .... (i)

26. math... matics .... (e)

27. ped....gogue .... (a)

28. sin....cure .... (e)

29. gutt....ral .... (u)

30. desp....rate .... (e)

31. sens....tive   .... (i)

32. compar....son   .... (i)

33. defin....tely   .... (i)

34. d....scription   .... (e)

35. compar....tive   .... (a)

36. rhinocer....s   .... (o)

37. syn....gogue   .... (a)

38. ind....scribable   .... (e)

IV. Write the complete word formed when -ABLE is added to each of the following:

1. notice

   ....   (noticeable)

2. desire

   ....   (desirable)

3. peace

   ....   (peaceable)

4. like

   ....   (likable)

5. excuse

   ....   (excusable)

6. love

   ....   (lovable)

7. enforce

   ....   (enforceable)

8. embrace

.... (embraceable)

9. size

.... (sizable)

10. pronounce

.... (pronounceable)

11. replace

.... (replaceable)

12. use

.... (usable)

13. service

.... (serviceable)

14. change

.... (changeable)

15. manage

.... (manageable)

16. prove

.... (provable)

17. value

.... (valuable)

18. marriage

.... (marriageable)

19. advise

.... (advisable)

20. exchange

.... (exchangeable)

21. live

.... (livable)

22. knowledge

.... (knowledgeable)

23. salvage

.... (salvageable)

24. move

.... (movable)

25. interchange

.... (interchangeable)

V. Add -ING to each of the following, writing the complete word.

1. ache

.... (aching)

2. advise

.... (advising)

3. hope

.... (hoping)

4. use

.... (using)

5. confuse

.... (confusing)

6. argue

.... (arguing)

7. arrive

.... (arriving)

8. desire

.... (desiring)

9. pare

.... (paring)

10. believe

.... (believing)

VI. Add the indicated suffix to each word, then rewrite the complete form. (Use preferable spellings only.)

1. DESIRE plus -OUS

.... (DESIROUS)

2. PORE plus -OUS

.... (POROUS)

3. ARGUE plus -ABLE

.... (ARGUABLE)

4. STONE plus -Y

.... (STONY)

5. BONE plus -Y

.... (BONY)

6. SPONGE plus -Y

.... (SPONGY)

7. STAGE plus -Y

.... (STAGY)

8. CAGE plus -Y

.... (CAGEY)

9. HOLE plus -Y

.... (HOLEY)

10. MERE plus -LY

.... (MERELY)

11. LONE plus -LY

.... (LONELY)

12. SINCERE plus -LY

.... (SINCERELY)

13. RARE plus -LY

.... (RARELY)

14. SOLE plus -LY

.... (SOLELY)

15. BARE plus -LY

.... (BARELY)

16. DECISIVE plus -LY

.... (DECISIVELY)

17. ADVERTISE plus -MENT

.... (ADVERTISEMENT)

18. EQUIP plus -MENT

.... (EQUIPMENT)

19. DEVELOP plus -MENT

.... (DEVELOPMENT)

20. EMBARRASS plus -MENT

.... (EMBARRASSMENT)

21. ENVELOP plus -MENT

.... (ENVELOPMENT)

22. HARASS plus -MENT

.... (HARASSMENT)

23. JUDGE plus -MENT

.... (JUDGMENT)

24. LODGE plus -MENT

.... (LODGMENT)

25. ABRIDGE plus -MENT

.... (ABRIDGMENT)

26. ACKNOWLEDGE plus -MENT

.... (ACKNOWLEDGMENT)

27. ARGUE plus -MENT

.... (ARGUMENT)

28. DUE plus -LY

.... (DULY)

29. TRUE plus -LY

.... (TRULY)

30. ONE plus -LY

.... (ONLY)

31. AWE plus -FUL

    ....   (AWFUL)

32. ACRE plus -AGE

    ....   (ACREAGE)

Chapter 24

-ABLE OR -IBLE? (I)

INDISPENS<u>ABLE</u> ends in -ABLE (though the average speller will either be confused or forthrightly—and incorrectly—write *indispensible*).

IRRESIST<u>IBLE</u> ends in -IBLE (though once again almost everyone but an expert will be tempted to write *irresistable*).

DEPEND<u>ABLE</u>, INIMIT<u>ABLE</u>, PREDICT<u>ABLE</u>, EXECR<u>ABLE</u> are -ABLE words; COLLAPS<u>IBLE</u>, CONTEMPT<u>IBLE</u>, CONNECT<u>IBLE</u> belong to the -IBLE group.

How is one ever to know which suffix is the proper one?

For the most part one relies on visual memory and luck —for -ABLE, -IBLE is probably the thorniest, most vexing, and most confusing problem in English spelling.

There are a few broad principles that can be followed— there are also a host of exceptions.

By learning to thread your way through the rules, and especially by strengthening your visual reactions to correct forms by intelligent practice, you, too, can become a near-expert in this puzzling category of commonly misspelled forms.

Let's examine the broad principles.

I. To begin with, there are more -ABLE than -IBLE words. If in doubt, use -ABLE.

II. Furthermore, if you start with any complete word, say PASS, WORK, BREAK, etc., the ending of choice is -ABLE: PASS<u>ABLE</u>, WORK<u>ABLE</u>, BREAK<u>ABLE</u>. (There *are* exceptions, however, as later chapters will show.)

Add -ABLE to the following full words, writing the complete forms in the blanks.

DEPEND	....	(DEPENDABLE)
EXPEND	....	(EXPENDABLE)
CORRECT	....	(CORRECTABLE)
PASS	....	(PASSABLE)
PROFIT	....	(PROFITABLE)
BREAK	....	(BREAKABLE)
AGREE	....	(AGREEABLE)
PREDICT	....	(PREDICTABLE)
PERISH	....	(PERISHABLE)
ACCEPT	....	(ACCEPTABLE)

No real problem yet. Start with a complete word, add -ABLE. Now, consider a third rule, very similar to the preceding one.

III. If a word ends in E preceded by a single consonant, drop E and add -ABLE, for example, PRESUME—PRESUMABLE, PLEASURE—PLEASURABLE.

Drop final -E and add -ABLE to the following, writing the complete form in the blanks.

DESIRE	....	(DESIRABLE)
DISPENSE	....	(DISPENSABLE)
PLEASURE	....	(PLEASURABLE)
BLAME	....	(BLAMABLE)
USE	....	(USABLE)
EXCUSE	....	(EXCUSABLE)

LOVE .... (LOV<u>ABLE</u>)

DEPLORE .... (DEPLOR<u>ABLE</u>)

COMPARE .... (COMPAR<u>ABLE</u>)

IV. But, as you recall from previous chapters, if your word ends in -CE or -GE, *retain* final E before adding -ABLE: NOTICE—NOTICEABLE, etc.

Add -ABLE to the following.

NOTICE .... (NOTIC<u>E</u>ABLE)

PEACE .... (PEAC<u>E</u>ABLE)

SERVICE .... (SERVIC<u>E</u>ABLE)

MARRIAGE .... (MARRIAG<u>E</u>ABLE)

V. We have already decided that the consonants C and G are "hard" (as in CAT and GASH) before the vowel A. Obviously, then, only -ABLE can follow a "hard" C or G. Rewrite the following, noting in each instance the pronunciation of the C or G.

INDEFATIG<u>ABLE</u>   ....

NAVIG<u>ABLE</u>   ....

APPLIC<u>ABLE</u>   ....

DESPIC<u>ABLE</u>   ....

EXPLIC<u>ABLE</u>   ....

AMIC<u>ABLE</u>   ....

IRREVOC<u>ABLE</u>   ....

IMPLAC<u>ABLE</u>   ....

VI. Following the letter I, only -ABLE can be used.

SOCI<u>ABLE</u>   ....

AMIABLE   ....

INSATIABLE   ....

RELIABLE   ....

ENVIABLE   ....

APPRECIABLE   ....

Well, that will get you started. The first six principles are
so simple they hardly bear repeating, but let's just run
through them quickly nevertheless.

   I. If in doubt, use -ABLE.
  II. Add -ABLE to most complete words.
 III. Add -ABLE to most words ending in E preceded by a
      single consonant, first, of course, dropping final E.
 IV. If a word ends in -CE or -GE, *retain* final E, then add
      -ABLE.
  V. Only -ABLE can follow "hard" C or G.
 VI. Only -ABLE can follow the vowel I.

Those are the simple rules. Tomorrow, we deal with a
more complicated principle governing -ABLE.

Chapter 25.

-ABLE OR -IBLE? (II)

So now let's consider IRRITABLE. How, aside from using -ABLE when in doubt, would we know to tack on the proper ending? There is no word *irrit-*, and we have no C, G, or I to point the way.

To decide that IRRITABLE ends in -ABLE we have to think of IRRITATE. To figure out the correct suffix for DEMONSTRABLE, we think of DEMONSTRATE; for IMPENETRABLE, PENETRATE; for ESTIMABLE, ESTIMATE; for TOLERABLE, TOLERATE; for INIMITABLE, IMITATE.

In short, if the root is followed by A in some other form of the word, the correct ending is -ABLE. In a chart, the principle looks like this:

ROOT	RELATED WORD	CORRECT ENDING
1. irrit-?	irritATE	irritABLE
2. demonstr-?	demonstrATE	demonstrABLE
3. impenetr-?	penetrATE	impenetrABLE
4. estim-?	estimATE	estimABLE
5. toler-?	tolerATE	tolerABLE
6. inimit-?	imitATE	inimitABLE

Try some on your own. I'll supply the root and the related word—you write the -ABLE form.

7. innumer-?	enumerATE	....
8. insepar-?	separATE	....

9. inviol-?   violATE   ....

10. commend-?   commendATION   ....

11. inflamm-?   inflammATION   ....

12. delect-?   delectATION   ....

13. irrepar-?   reparATION   ....

14. dur-?   durATION   ....

15. impregn-?   pregnANT   ....

16. cap-?   capACITY   ....

Some -ABLE forms do not fit into any of our five specific principles. They can be governed by our general principle (if in doubt, use -ABLE), but let's practice on the few that might tempt to misspelling.

Try writing the following:

17. FORMIDABLE   ....

18. EQUITABLE   ....

19. INEVITABLE   ....

20. CULPABLE   ....

21. INDOMITABLE   ....

22. INSUPERABLE   ....

23. INEFFABLE   ....

24. INSCRUTABLE   ....

25. VULNERABLE   ....

26. INEXORABLE   ....

27. AFFABLE   ....

28. PORTABLE   ....

29. UNCONSCIONABLE   ....

Before turning to the principles governing words ending in -IBLE, let us check your understanding of the -ABLE rules:

1. Generally, -ABLE is added to a complete

   ....   (word)

2. If a word ends in E preceded by a

   ...., drop E and add -ABLE.   (consonant)

3. If a word ends in -CE or -GE, however,

   .... final -E before adding -ABLE.   (retain)

4. -ABLE is always used after the

   vowel .....   (I)

5. Also after "........" C.   (hard)

6. And after "hard" .....   (G)

7. If the root is followed by ....   (A)

   in some other form of the word,

   the ending is -ABLE.

8. Otherwise, if in doubt, use ....   (-ABLE)

Chapter 26

-ABLE OR -IBLE? (III)

So that takes care of -ABLE. How about -IBLE?
Again, we can follow some fairly clear-cut principles.

I. We have said that -ABLE is added to a complete word.
It would logically follow, then, that -IBLE is added to a
root that is *not* a complete word. Consider the following
roots, notice that none are complete words, then add -IBLE,
and rewrite.

1. cred........

    ....

2. aud........

    ....

3. ed........

    ....

4. divis........

    ....

5. feas........

    ....

6. plaus........

    ....

7. vis........

    ....

8. ris........

    ....

9. combust........

    ....

10. suscept........

    ....

11. compat........   14. poss........

....

12. terr........   15. indel........

....

13. horr........   16. infall........

....

II. -ABLE follows "hard" G, as in NAVIGABLE or INDEFATIGABLE. This we already know. Therefore, if the G preceding the suffix is "soft," like the G in GIN, we must use -IBLE, as in NEGLIG<u>IBLE</u> and INTELLI-<u>GIBLE</u>.

Rewrite the following, noting that the G has a "soft," or J, sound.

17. negli*gible*   19. eli*gible*

....

18. intelli*gible*   20. tan*gible*

....

III. You will recall that certain words ending in -CE, for instance NOTICE and SERVICE, retain final E preceding -ABLE. Certain other words, notably those ending in -NCE, -UCE, and -RCE, drop final E, but keep C "soft" by using -IBLE, since C has the sound of S before I, as in CITY or CINCH.

Drop final E, add -IBLE, and rewrite the complete word. Note that each root ends in -NCE, -UCE, or -RCE.

21. convince   22. induce

....

23. reduce   25. force

....

24. produce

....

IV. Certain forms do not derive from -CE words; the -IBLE is nevertheless necessary in order to keep the preceding C "soft."

26. invincible   28. miscible

....

27. irascible

....

V. The ending is -IBLE whenever the root ends in MISS-:

29. per*missible*   31. dis*missible*

....

30. trans*missible*   32. ad*missible*

....

VI. A root that ends in -NS also takes -IBLE:

33. comprehe*nsible*   35. oste*nsible*

....

34. expa*nsible*   36. defe*nsible*

....

Note, however, that two important exceptions end in -ABLE: DISPENS<u>ABLE</u> and INDISPENS<u>ABLE</u>.

So let's review our six new principles by asking you to check on your learning.

1. -IBLE is the proper suffix when the root

   is not a .... word.   (complete)

2. For example, the root of VISIBLE is

   ...., which is not a complete word.   (vis-)

3. -IBLE is the proper suffix after a

   "........" G or C.   (soft)

4. In INTELLIGIBLE, for example, the

   G preceding -IBLE is pronounced

   like a .....   (J)

5. If a word ends in -NCE, -RCE, or ....,   (-UCE)

   drop final E and add -IBLE.

6. Roots similar to that of PERMISSIBLE,

   i.e., ending in ...., take -IBLE.   (-MISS)

7. Roots like that of DEFENSIBLE, i.e.,

   ending in ...., take -IBLE.   (-NS)

8. The two important exceptions to

   the foregoing are: ....   (DISPENSABLE,

   ....   INDISPENSABLE)

Chapter 27.
-ABLE OR -IBLE? (IV)

Again, as with -ABLE, we have first studied the simple principles. Now we are ready to consider something more complex.

Do you recall that we used -ABLE after IRRIT- to form IRRIT<u>ABLE</u> because of the related word IRRIT<u>A</u>TE, in which A followed the root?

We have a similar gimmick for certain -IBLE forms.

Consider COLLECT<u>IBLE</u>. Though the root is COLLECT, a complete word, we nevertheless violate one of our -ABLE principles because there is a related word, COLLECT<u>I</u>ON, in which I follows the root.

Consider the following:

ROOT	RELATED WORD	CORRECT ENDING
1. collect-?	collectION	collectIBLE
2. access-?	accessION	accessIBLE
3. contract-?	contractION	contractIBLE
4. suppress-?	suppressION	suppressIBLE
5. repress-?	repressION	repressIBLE
6. exhaust-?	exhaustION	exhaustIBLE

How shall we phrase our seventh rule?

VII. If, in a related word, -ION immediately follows the root, -IBLE is the correct ending.

BUT . . .

Three important words are exceptions: CORRECT<u>ABLE</u>, DETECT<u>ABLE</u>, and PREDICT<u>ABLE</u> end in -ABLE despite the related forms CORRECTION, DETECTION, PREDICTION.

Keep these three in mind; practice them below to get a firm grasp of them.

7. CORRECT<u>ABLE</u>   9. PREDICT<u>ABLE</u>

....

8. DETECT<u>ABLE</u>

....

Sometimes terminal D or T of a root will change to S before the -ION of a related form. For instance:

ROOT	RELATED WORD	CORRECT ENDING
10. corrod-?	corroSION	corrodIBLE
11. erod-?	eroSION	erodIBLE
12. convert-?	converSION	convertIBLE
13. pervert-?	perverSION	pervertIBLE

We have a last, or eighth, category that will finish our work with -ABLE, -IBLE forms, a category comprised of six words that are exceptions to an early -ABLE principle.

We learned, you will remember, that a complete word, or a word ending in E preceded by a single consonant, takes -ABLE: REMARK—REMARKABLE; PRESUME —PRESUMABLE.

In this final group are six special complete words which add -IBLE, not -ABLE.

Become thoroughly familiar with the following; rewrite each -IBLE form.

14. resist—RESIST<u>IBLE</u>   ....

15. discern—DISCERN<u>IBLE</u>   ....

16. gull—GULL<u>IBLE</u>   ....

17. contempt—CONTEMPT<u>IBLE</u>   ....

18. flex—FLEX<u>IBLE</u>   ....

19. collapse—COLLAPS<u>IBLE</u>   ....

Needless to say, the negatives of the preceding adjectives end the same way. Practice these:

20. IRRESISTIBLE ....

21. UNDISCERNIBLE ....

22. INFLEXIBLE ....

A Thought for Tomorrow

Are you ready now for a thorough review of all the principles we have been studying? In the next chapter you will realize that you are now close to becoming an expert on -ABLE, -IBLE forms.

Chapter 28.

COMPLETE REVIEW ON -ABLE, -IBLE

English spelling, bear in mind, does not follow rules.

It's the other way around, as we have already learned.

If we consider a large body of related words, we can formulate certain principles that serve to explain, or perhaps even justify, their patterns; with, usually, a number of exceptions left over that won't fit into the Procrustean bed we have devised.

And this is precisely what we have been up to in solving our -ABLE, -IBLE problems. We've considered the words, drawn up specific principles, and added certain exceptions.

Let us take a final look at these principles, illustrating each with new examples, for, of course, we have dealt with only a portion of all the -ABLE, -IBLE words that occur in English.

I. When the root is *a complete word,* generally the ending is -ABLE.

Complete the following, then rewrite:

1. disagree........

   ....

2. bear........

   ....

3. present........

   ....

4. person........

   ....

5. pardon........

   ....

II. When the root is a complete word ending in E preceded by a single consonant, drop terminal E and add -ABLE.

Add -ABLE to the following:

6. live   9. love

....

7. presume   10. like

....

8. adore

....

III. If a word ends in -CE or -GE, retain the E before adding -ABLE.

Add -ABLE to these:

11. replace   14. abridge

....

12. trace   15. salvage

....

13. expunge

....

IV. Only -ABLE may follow a "hard" C or G.

Add -ABLE to the following:

16. communic........   18. impractic........

....

17. ineradic........   19. unnavig........

....

20. irrefrag........

....

V. Only -ABLE may follow the vowel I.
   Add -ABLE to the following:

21. vari........   23. justifi........

....

22. classifi........

....

VI. -ABLE is used if the root is followed by A in a related form.
   Add -ABLE to the following, noting the related form in
parentheses:

24. inhabit........   (inhabitANT)   ....

25. inoper........   (operATE)   ....

26. hospit........   (hospitALITY)   ....

27. execr........   (execrATE)   ....

28. abomin........   (abominATE)   ....

VII. Certain -ABLE words fit into no serviceable category.
    Complete the following:

29. inevit........   31. inequit........

....

30. tract........

....

VIII. Generally, if a root is not a complete word, -IBLE
is the correct suffix.
   Complete these:

32. incred........   34. ined........

....

33. incompat........   35. inaud........

....

IX. -IBLE follows "soft" G.
   Do these:

36. leg........   38. inelig........

....

37. incorrig........   39. intang........

....

X. -IBLE also follows "soft" C, particularly -RC, -NC,
and -UC.
   Complete the following:

40. coerc........   42. unconvinc........

....

41. seduc........   43. irasc........

....

XI. -IBLE follows MISS- and NS-, except for DISPENS-
ABLE and INDISPENSABLE.
   Complete the following:

44. inadmiss........   46. reprehens........

....

45. incomprehens........   47. respons........

....

48. sens........

....

XII. If, in a related form, -ION immediately follows the root (even though D or T may change to S), -IBLE is the correct suffix. But CORRECTABLE, DETECTABLE, and PREDICTABLE are exceptions.
   Complete these:

49. express........   (expressION) ....

50. impress........   (impressION).......................................

51. digest........   (digestION) ....

52. perfect........   (perfectION) ....

53. revers........   (reversION) ....

54. corrupt........   (corruptION) ....

55. destruct ....   (destructION).......................................

XIII. And again, certain -IBLE words fit into no definite category, or seem to be exceptions to previous rules.
   Complete these:

56. resist........   60. flex........

....

57. discern........   61. collapse........

....

58. gull........   62. irresist........

....

59. contempt........   63. undiscern........

....

64. inflex........

....

Are you still with me? Then write in each blank whether a root calls for -ABLE or -IBLE.

1. Root is followed by A in related
   form (DUR-).

   ....   (-ABLE)

2. -ION directly follows root in related
   form (DESTRUCT-).

   ....   (-IBLE)

3. Complete word (CONQUER-).

   ....   (-ABLE)

4. Complete word ending in E preceded
   by a single consonant (PRESUME-).

   ....   (-ABLE)

5. Root not a complete word (CRED-).

   ....   (-IBLE)

6. Ends in "hard" C (COMMUNIC-).

   ....   (-ABLE)

7. Root ends in "soft" C, especially
   -NC, -RC, or -UC (IRREDUC-).

   ....   (-IBLE)

8. Ends in "hard" G (NAVIG-).

   ....   (-ABLE)

9. Root ends in "soft" G (LEG-).

....   (-IBLE)

10. Ends in I (APPRECI-).

....   (-ABLE)

11. Root ends in -MISS (INADMISS-).

....   (-IBLE)

12. Root ends in -NS (INDEFENS-).

....   (-IBLE)

Chapter 29.

"MULTIPLE REPRESENTATION"

The sound of J is represented, in English, by the letter J (JAM, JELLY, etc.); by the letter G (GEM, GENTLE, etc.); or sometimes by the letters DG (ABRIDGE, KNOWLEDGE, etc.).

This "multiple representation" is what makes our spelling so hard a nut to crack.

Generally, a literate person can take the wealth of choices in his stride—sometimes, however, he is faced with an embarrassment of riches.

And so, long accustomed to prefixing a D to a G when the preceding vowel has a short sound (as in JUDGE, LODGE, BLUDGEON, BRIDGE, RIDGE, BADGE, WEDGE, LEDGE, and many others), he often gets confused when he has to write a word like ALLEGE or PRIVILEGE, in which no D is required.

So let's get squared away on those words in which the G needs no help from any outside source.

Words for Today

Note particularly that the G in each word below is *not* preceded by a D; then cover it and rewrite. Note, also, the difference in the order of the vowels E and I in the words RELIGION and RELIGIOUS on the one hand, and SACRILEGE, SACRILEGIOUS, and PRIVILEGE on the other.

1. RELIGION ....

2. RELIGIOUS ....

3. SACRILEGE   ....

4. SACRILEGIOUS   ....

5. PRIVILEGE   ....

6. ALLEGE   ....

7. PIGEON   ....

Sidelights

Perhaps the spelling of SACRILEGIOUS was a surprise to
you—every person I know spells it as if it were the word
RELIGIOUS with a prefix tacked on, unless someone has
called the correct form to his attention. And the common
pronunciation SAK-re-LIJ-us is no help either.

But let's examine the derivation of the word. The Latin
verb *legere,* to gather up or take away (COLLECT comes
from another form of this verb), combines with the Latin
adjective *sacris,* sacred, to form *sacrilegus,* one who gathers
up and takes away sacred objects, in short a temple-robber.
And so the *sacri-* plus the *leg-* give us SACRILEGE, the
noun, or by the addition of -IOUS, SACRILEGIOUS, the
adjective, both with the -ILE-, not -ELI-, pattern.

In the case of PRIVILEGE we have a somewhat dif-
ferent derivation, despite the similarity in spelling pattern.
Latin *lex, legis,* law (from which we get LEGAL and LEG-
ISLATE) combines with *privus,* separate or special—a
PRIVILEGE is a special law not made for everyone.

Note also the following the G in RELIGION, RELI-
GIOUS and SACRILEGIOUS; without it, G would be
"hard" before O, as in GONE.

The -E in PIGEON serves to keep the G "soft"—it
would otherwise be hard before O, as in GO, GONE, or
RAGOUT. This spelling refers, of course, to the bird, and
should not be confused with the PIDGIN in *pidgin English,*
a jargon used in the South Pacific islands by the natives
and the Chinese in their dealings with foreigners. PIDGIN
itself is a corruption of the Chinese pronunciation of the
English word BUSINESS—so *pidgin English* is literally

BUSINESS ENGLISH, though not the kind taught in the local high school.

More Words for Today

While we are talking about not using unnecessary letters, we might consider four words in which poor spellers tend to insert a superfluous S.

1. OCCASIONAL. *Pleasure, measure,* and *treasure* are rarely misspelled—it seems supremely reasonable to represent the middle consonant sound (represented in dictionaries by ZH) with a single S. In OCCASION and OCCASIONAL we have the same sound, the same single S. Why poor spellers tend to double the S is still a mystery to me, but the fact is that they do.

   Write the word: ....

2. PASTIME. An activity engaged in mainly to *pass time* pleasantly is called a PASTIME. There should, logically, be two S's, everything in the derivation calls for two S's (the word is a translation of French *passe-temps*), but logic, as we have long since learned, does not always have a strong influence on English spelling. Use one S only.

   Write the word: ....

3. TRESPASS. This word comes from Latin *transpassare,* pass across—change the first vowel, drop a few letters here and there, and we have the English word so often misspelled with an uncalled-for double S in the middle.

   Write the word: ....

4. OBEISANCE. Here, again, since the S has a sharp, or hissed, sound as in TRESPASS, there is a great temptation, even among the literate, to add an extra S for good measure. Be less generous—use one S only.

   Write the word: ....

Still More Words

So, away with superfluous D's, G's, and S's. Let us also get rid of a couple of B's, though we'll be defying all the laws of logic in doing so.

B is a kind of silent finishing touch on many words—DUMB, NUMB, THUMB, LIMB, etc. It looks so odd hanging off the end of each word, and is so unnecessary in pronunciation, that everyone remembers without difficulty to add it on.

Now, if you CONFOUND someone so completely that you strike him DUMB, wouldn't it make sense to spell it DUMBFOUND? It would, and this spelling is technically correct—but (hold your hat) DUMFOUND is far preferable. (Why? Sometimes there's no reason, and this is one of those times.)

Also, if you're so stupid that your SKULL is NUMB, you're a NUMBSKULL, no? No. You're a NUMSKULL, the logical spelling not even being technically correct. Again, no reason.

However, don't despair. Here's your B back after an M. Many writers, paradoxically enough, either forget the B at the end of SUCCUM<u>B</u> or feel unsure after they've put it on. But it belongs in all forms—SUCCUMBED, SUCCUMBING, etc. And note that U is the only vowel in the original verb: SUCCU<u>MB</u>.

Let's look at a few more contradictions. A<u>GG</u>RESSIVE has a double G. A<u>G</u>REE (also the negative DISA<u>G</u>REE) has a single G. Yet the sound is the same.

SU<u>P</u>ERCILIOUS, SU<u>P</u>ERFICIAL, SU<u>P</u>ERIMPOSE, SU<u>P</u>ERINTEND, and similar words have one P—they derive from Latin *super*, above, and the U preceding the P has a sound approximating that of the OO in FOOD.

On the other hand, SU<u>PP</u>RESS, SU<u>PP</u>ORT, and SU<u>P</u>POSE have double P's—the derivation in these words is from Latin *sub*, under (the B of *sub-* changes to a P when the prefix is combined with a root that starts with a P), and now the U has a slightly more rounded sound.

There are those who are sometimes puzzled whether to

use one or two P's after a U. Generally, the sound of the U is the key: long, as in FOOD, one P; rounded, two P's. The derivation, as described above, is even more helpful, but not everyone is an amateur etymologist.

Let's Practice

So let's see what we've covered today.
—Certain words are spelled G, not DG (ALLEGE, etc.).
—Certain words have one S where an insecure speller might generously use two (OCCASIONAL, etc.).
—Two words that should logically have a B, don't (DUM-FOUND, NUMSKULL).
—In certain words a G or a P is doubled (AGGRESSIVE, SUPPRESS), in others it is not (AGREE, SUPERB).

Attack today's words once again, refreshing your visual memory of those parts that are tricky, then cover and write each one correctly.

RELIGION   ....

RELIGIOUS   ....

SACRILEGE   ....

SACRILEGIOUS   ....

PRIVILEGE   ....

ALLEGE   ....

PIGEON   ....

PIDGIN   ....

OCCASION   ....

OCCASIONAL   ....

PASTIME   ....

TRESPASS   ....

OBEISANCE   ....

DU<u>MF</u>OUND   ....

NU<u>MS</u>KULL   ....

SU<u>CCU</u>MB   ....

A<u>GG</u>RESSIVE   ....

A<u>G</u>REE   ....

DISA<u>G</u>REE   ....

SU<u>PP</u>RESS   ....

SU<u>PP</u>ORT   ....

SU<u>PP</u>OSE   ....

More Practice

Can you respond meaningfully by completing each statement below? Deciding which word is required will be easy —spelling it correctly may be another story.

  1. A stupid person is a

    (N-) ....   (NU<u>MS</u>KULL)

  2. If you say "yes," you

    (A-) ....   (A<u>G</u>REE)

  3. If you say "no," you

    (D-) ....   (DISA<u>G</u>REE)

  4. Christianity is a

    (R-) ....   (RE<u>LI</u>GION)

  5. Voting is a

    (P-) ....   (PRIV<u>IL</u>EGE)

  6. A certain bird is called a
    homing

    (P-) ....   (PI<u>GE</u>ON)

7. A South Pacific dialect is

(P-) .... English (PIDGIN)

8. A pious person is

(R-) .... (RELIGIOUS)

9. A profane or impious person is

(S-) .... (SACRILEGIOUS)

10. He commits

(S-) .... (SACRILEGE)

11. To astonish is to

(D-) .... (DUMFOUND)

12. To go where you don't belong is to

(T-) .... (TRESPASS)

13. You are then a

(T-) .... (TRESPASSER)

14. An amusement is also called a

(P-) .... (PASTIME)

15. A gesture of respect is an

(O-) .... (OBEISANCE)

16. To give in, die, etc. is to

(S-) .... (SUCCUMB)

17. An active, energetic person is usually

(A-) .... (AGGRESSIVE)

18. To hold back is to

    (S-) .... (SUPPRESS)

19. To state without legal
    proof is to

    (A-) .... (ALLEGE)

20. Marriage is an important

    (O-) .... in a woman's   (OCCASION)
    life

21. An adverb meaning *once
    in a while* is

    (O-) .... (OCCASIONALLY)

22. To believe, decide, or
    imagine is to

    (S-) .... (SUPPOSE)

23. To hold up is to

    (S-) .... (SUPPORT)

A Thought for Tomorrow

Is STATIONERY the only way to spell the word? Is there another spelling for PRINCIPLE? How about CORD?

Chapter 30.
HOMONYMS

Homonyms are words that sound alike but are spelled differently—for example, BARE and BEAR, WAIT and WEIGHT, PALE and PAIL, etc.

Most homonyms cause no difficulty—literate people correctly differentiate between GRATE and GREAT or GROAN and GROWN without a second thought; they never write "He had a *soar* on his foot," or "The plane *sored* aloft."

So, though there are hundreds of sets of exact or approximate homonyms, only a few offer a fertile field for confusion. Let's look at the ten that are most confusing.

1. PRINCIPLE—PRINCIPAL

Any rule, truth, or pattern of conduct is spelled PRINCIPLE—note that RULE and PRINCIPLE have the same endings. PRINCIPLE is a noun only.

For any other meaning, adjective or noun, spell it PRINCIPAL. The PRINCIPAL of a school; the PRINCIPAL on which banks pay interest; the PRINCIPALS in play, in business negotiations, or in any other activity—all end in -AL. The adjective, meaning *main* or *chief,* is always PRINCIPAL—the PRINCIPAL facts, reasons, resources, industries, etc. In all these uses PRINCIPAL in some way conveys the idea of MAIN—note the A in both words.

So . . .

He is a man of PRINCIPLE.

There are certain PRINCIPLES of spelling.

He is an UNPRINCIPLED scoundrel.

New York is the PRINCIPAL city on the East Coast.

2. STATIONARY—STATIONERY
STATIONARY is an adjective meaning unmoving, fixed, attached, standing still, etc.

STATIONERY is a noun meaning PAPER (note the -ER in both words) and other supplies or implements for writing.

3. CHORD—CORD
A CHORD refers to music, emotion, or a geometric figure. You hit a CHORD on the piano; he broke one of the CHORDS on his harp; Marilyn Monroe struck a responsive CHORD in male breasts; CHORD AB intersects the circle at O.

A CORD is a length of string, twine, or rope, or anything so shaped, including the vocal CORDS.

4. PORE—POUR
You PORE over something you're reading or studying —you POUR milk into a pitcher.

5. FLAIR—FLARE
You have a FLAIR, i.e., a natural talent, for art, writing, music, etc.

Otherwise, the spelling is FLARE—a person FLARES up in anger, a skirt FLARES out, a runway is lighted by FLARES, etc.

6. FAINT—FEINT
You feel FAINT, or you FAINT at the sight of blood; but a prizefighter FEINTS with his left (and then delivers a haymaker with his right, having caught his opponent off guard), or you make a FEINT (i.e., a pretense) of working when the boss is around. FEINT, of course, comes from the verb FEIGN, to pretend.

7. CANON—CANNON
With one N—CANON—the word has various meanings in reference to the church: a clergyman, church law, etc.; or is a standard of judgment.

With a double N—CANNON—the word designates

a very large, nonportable military gun, or artillery collectively (it is both a singular and plural word in this meaning); or the part by which a bell is hung.

Various derivative forms, then—CANONIZE, CANONICALS, CANONESS; CANNONADE, CANNONEER—will have one N or two depending on the meaning of the root form.

He is a CANON of the Anglican Church.

He is an authority on Roman Catholic CANON.

There were certain CANONS of good taste he never violated.

The CANNON boomed all day.

8. BAITED—BATED

BAITED is the past tense of the verb BAIT to tease or to tempt or entice—he BAITED his wife unmercifully, BAITED the trap, etc.

BATED is the correct spelling in the phrase "with BATED breath"—it comes from the verb BATE, to hold in.

9. DESERT—DESSERT

With one S the word means an arid region, such as the Gobi DESERT. It is, of course, also a verb meaning to abandon, forsake, etc.

With two S's, it's the ice cream, pudding, cake, pie, etc., that tops off a meal.

DESERT (i.e., the Sahara) is accented on the first syllable; the verb to DESERT is accented on the second syllable, as is also the noun DESSERT.

10. CANVAS—CANVASS

CANVAS (one S) is a kind of cloth; CANVASS (two S's) is a verb meaning to solicit orders, votes, opinions, information, etc., or a noun with the corresponding meaning—to CANVASS the neighborhood, conduct a CANVASS, etc.

Check Your Learning
Which word correctly completes each sentence?

1. His (PRINCIPAL, PRINCIPLE)
   interest in life is eating.   (PRINCIPAL)

2. He lives by strict (PRINCIPALS,
   PRINCIPLES).   (PRINCIPLES)

3. Lola Albright plays one of the
   (PRINCIPAL, PRINCIPLE) roles
   in "Cold Wind in August."   (PRINCIPAL)

4. Miss Albright is a (PRINCIPAL,
   PRINCIPLE) in the movie.   (PRINCIPAL)

5. Banks now pay 4% on your
   (PRINCIPAL, PRINCIPLE).   (PRINCIPAL)

6. It's not the money, it's the
   (PRINCIPAL, PRINCIPLE) of
   the thing.   (PRINCIPLE)

7. We are running low on (STATION-
   ARY, STATIONERY).   (STATIONERY)

8. This house does not have (STA-
   TIONARY, STATIONERY) walls.   (STATIONARY)

9. His vocal (CORDS, CHORDS)
   are inflamed.   (CORDS)

10. Children strike a responsive
    (CORD, CHORD) in most
    women.   (CHORD)

11. Tie the package with stout (CORD,
    CHORD).   (CORD)

12. He banged out a few (CORDS,
    CHORDS) on the piano.   (CHORDS)

13. He stayed up all night (PORING,
    POURING) over his income-tax
    return.   (PORING)

14. He has quite a (FLARE, FLAIR)
    for dramatics.   (FLAIR)

15. She was wearing a (FLAIRED,
    FLARED) skirt.   (FLARED)

16. (FAINT, FEINT) heart never won
    fair woman.   (FAINT)

17. The army made a (FAINT, FEINT) to the north. (FEINT)

18. The roar of the (CANON, CANNON) was deafening. (CANNON)

19. In good writing, certain literary (CANONS, CANNONS) are observed. (CANONS)

20. Only a few women have been (CANONIZED, CANNONIZED) by the Roman Catholic Church. (CANONIZED)

21. They watched with (BAITED, BATED) breath. (BATED)

22. Stop (BATING, BAITING) me. (BAITING)

23. Would you like some (DESERT, DESSERT)? (DESSERT)

24. They slept under (CANVAS, CANVASS) for two weeks. (CANVAS)

25. Have you conducted a (CANVAS, CANVASS) of the teachers' reactions to the new schedule? (CANVASS)

Chapter 31

MISCELLANEOUS TRAPS AND
HOW TO AVOID THEM

Some words are just difficult to spell no matter how good you are—for example, the thirty we shall struggle with today.

But, oddly enough, and as you have already discovered for yourself, concentrating on the particular areas that make them difficult, forming a strong visual image of the pattern of letters in those areas, and writing them two or three times in meaningful situations, serve almost magically to make you master of them.

Consider, then, the following. Study the underlined letters, read any explanatory notes, then cover each word and rewrite it.

1. B<u>U</u>SINE<u>SS</u>

   This may not be one of your pet misspellings—in which case, you'd probably be surprised how many people write it as *buisness,* which after all does get all the letters in, and is much closer to the pronunciation. The word is, of course, BUSY plus -NESS, the Y changed to I.

   Write the word: ....

2. A<u>M</u>ONG

   And this demon, by analogy with YOUNG, is often misspelled *amoung.* Poor spellers, as I have said, enjoy slipping in unnecessary letters out of misbegotten generosity.

   Write the word: ....

3. **DISHEVELED**
This is not *sheveled* plus DIS-; so only one S.

Write the word: ....

4. **THRESHOLD**
And this is *not* THRESH plus HOLD; so only one H after the S.

Write the word: ....

5. **WITHHOLD**
But this *is* WITH plus HOLD—*two* H's.

Write the word: ....

6. **FOURTEEN**
FOUR plus TEEN.

Write the word: ....

7. **FORTY**
Not FOUR plus -TY— *no* U.

Write the word: ....

8. **GRATEFUL**
No relationship to GREAT; the word comes from the Latin *gratus,* pleasing or thankful, and is related to GRATITUDE, GRATIS, and CONGRATULATE.

Write the word: ....

9. **HIPPOPOTAMUS**
If you pronounce the word carefully you'll get all the letters in their correct place, including the -US ending, even though RHINOCEROS, as we know, ends in -OS.

Write the word: ....

10. **HAREBRAINED**
Describes a person (or his actions, ideas, etc.) who has the brain of a HARE, i.e., a rabbit, not who has HAIR on his brain. Perhaps HARES are smarter than we

think and we are unnecessarily maligning them.

Write the word: ....

11. KIMON̲O

We say ki-MO-na, but the last letter is an O.

Write the word: ....

12. K̲HAKI

The H follows the initial K.

Write the word: ....

13. NICKEL̲

Unlike PICKLE, PRICKLE, SICKLE, and similar words, NICKEL ends in -EL, whether five cents or the metal.

Write the word: ....

14. PRONUN̲CIATION

The verb is PRONOUNCE, but the noun (often mis-pronounced, by the way) is correctly spelled (and said) without the O after the first N.

Write the word: ....

15. MINER̲ALOGY

Most sciences end in -OLOGY (ANTHROPOLOGY, BIOLOGY, CYTOLOGY, etc.), but the science of MINER̲ALS ends in -AL̲OGY.

Write the word: ....

Let's pause at the halfway mark to give you further practice in getting the better of these nasty little words. Write the word we have studied that fits each definition—initial letters will guide you to the proper term.

1. A wrapper

(K-) ....   (KIMONO)

2. Big, thick-skinned beast

    (H-) .... (HIPPOPOTAMUS)

3. The number after 39

    (F-) .... (FORTY)

4. The number after 13

    (F-) .... (FOURTEEN)

5. In the midst of

    (A-) .... (AMONG)

6. A light brown color

    (K-) .... (KHAKI)

7. Five cents

    (N-) .... (NICKEL)

8. Science of minerals

    (M-) .... (MINERALOGY)

9. Stupid

    (H-) .... (HAREBRAINED)

10. Way of saying words

    (P-) .... (PRONUNCIATION)

11. Thankful

    (G-) .... (GRATEFUL)

12. Unkempt; with one's clothes
    and hair awry

    (D-) .... (DISHEVELED)

13. Hold back

(W-) .... (WITHHOLD)

14. Beginning; doorsill

(T-) .... (THRESHOLD)

15. Commercial affairs

(B-) .... (BUSINESS)

The misspellings of many of the words we are considering today make more sense than the correct spelling—at least to those who misspell them. If this applies to you, you must go through a kind of relearning, see a new and better kind of logic in the correct patterns, and train your visual and muscular memory to reject the form you were once so fond of. So let's proceed.

16. STRAIT JACKET
Its purpose is *not* to keep your body STRAIGHT; the first part comes from the same root as STRAIN, and means tight or narrow.

Write the word: ....

17. VIOLONCELLO
It looks like a big VIOLIN, but notice the O where most people expect an I. The derivation is Italian *violone*, a bass viol.

Write the word: ....

18. YEOMAN
The sound of the first syllable is *yoe*, but the correct spelling transposes the two vowels.

Write the word: ....

19. SOLDER
This is pronounced *sodder* but isn't written that way.

It comes from the same Latin root that gives us the English word SOLID, hence the L.

Write the word: ....

20. VICTUALS
Pronounced *vittles* but again not so spelled. From a Latin verb *vivere, victus,* to live—and VICTUALS sustain life in us.

Write the word: ....

21. RHYTHM
Most spellers tend to ignore the first H.

Write the word: ....

22. PARAFFIN
Like TARIFF and SHERIFF, it has one R and two F's.

Write the word: ....

23. GENEALOGY
Like MINERALOGY, it ends in -ALOGY. Pronounce it right and you'll spell it right (though in many other words, pronunciation serves only to lead you astray).

Write the word: ....

24. MANUFACTURE
Here again, correct pronunciation indicates the correct letter. From the same root as MANUSCRIPT (written by hand) and MANUAL (pertaining to the hand), MANUFACTURE etymologically means making by hand, though the machine age changed all that. But note the U following N in all three words. (The Latin for hand is *manus.*)

Write the word: ....

25. PERSPIRATION
Correct pronunciation will again indicate that the first

syllable is PER-, *not* PRES-. To PERSPIRE is to breathe (Latin *spiro*) through (Latin *per-*) the pores.

Write the word: ....

26. PRESCRIPTION
But here the first syllable *is* PRE-, and once more the correct pronunciation guides you to the proper letters. From Latin *scriptus*, written, plus *pre-*, before.

Write the word: ....

27. PROTUBERANT
Anything PROTUBERANT protrudes, so the misspelling with the extra R is quite understandable. But this word is from Latin *tuber*, a bump or bulge.

Write the word: ....

28. SMOOTH (verb)
Illogical, in a way, since the verb SOOTHE has a final E. But whether adjective or verb, this word has no E.

Write the word: ....

29. REPETITION
It sounds as if the underlined letter should be an I (and a poor speller invariably so writes it), but think that the verb from which this noun comes is REPEAT.

Write the word: ....

30. COMPETITION
Same principle—from the verb COMPETE.
Write the word: ....

Ready for some more practice? Write the word that fits each definition.

16. Food

(V-) ....   (VICTUALS)

17. Petty officer in the U.S. Navy

(Y-) ....   (YEOMAN)

18. Restraining jacket

(S-) ....   (STRAIT JACKET)

19. To make

(M-) ....   (MANUFACTURE)

20. To make smooth

(S-) ....   (SMOOTH)

21. Cello

(V-) ....   (VIOLONCELLO)

22. To fuse two metals

(S-) ....   (SOLDER)

23. Act of competing

(C-) ....   (COMPETITION)

24. Act of saying again

(R-) ....   (REPETITION)

25. Family tree

(G-) ....   (GENEALOGY)

26. A kind of wax

(P-) ....   (PARAFFIN)

27. Measured beat

(R-) ....   (RHYTHM)

28. Sweat

(P-) ....   (PERSPIRATION)

29. Protruding

   (P-) ....   (PROTUBERANT)

30. Doctor's order for drugs

   (P-) ....   (PRESCRIPTION)

Really expert on these 30 words now?

Prove it by rewriting each one correctly—all the following forms are deliberately misspelled.

1. amoung

   ....   (AMONG)

2. disshevelled

   ....   (DISHEVELED)

3. threshhold

   ....   (THRESHOLD)

4. buisness

   ....   (BUSINESS)

5. withold

   ....   (WITHHOLD)

6. forteen

   ....   (FOURTEEN)

7. fourty

   ....   (FORTY)

8. greatful

   ....   (GRATEFUL)

9. hippopotamos

....   (HIPPOPOTAMUS)

10. hairbrained

....   (HAREBRAINED)

11. kimona

....   (KIMONO)

12. kakhi

....   (KHAKI)

13. nickle

....   (NICKEL)

14. pronounciation

....   (PRONUNCIATION)

15. minerology

....   (MINERALOGY)

16. straight jacket

....   (STRAIT JACKET)

17. violincello

....   (VIOLONCELLO)

18. yoeman

....   (YEOMAN)

19. sodder

....   (SOLDER)

20. vittles

....   (VICTUALS)

21. rythm

.... (RHYTHM)

22. parrafin

.... (PARAFFIN)

23. geneology

.... (GENEALOGY)

24. manafacture

.... (MANUFACTURE)

25. prespiration

.... (PERSPIRATION)

26. perscription

.... (PRESCRIPTION)

27. protruberant

.... (PROTUBERANT)

28. smoothe (verb)

.... (SMOOTH)

29. repitition

.... (REPETITION)

30. compitition

.... (COMPETITION)

Chapter 32

FOURTH REVIEW TEST

I. Add either -ABLE or -IBLE to each root, then rewrite the complete word.

1. depend........   .... (able)

2. cred........   .... (ible)

3. plaus........   .... (ible)

4. correct........   .... (able)

5. accept........   .... (able)

6. infall........   .... (ible)

7. predict........   .... (able)

8. indispens........   .... (able)

9. excus........   .... (able)

10. irreduc........   .... (ible)

11. service........   .... (able)

12. irrit........   .... (able)

13. admiss........   .... (ible)

14. inimit........   .... (able)

15. ineff........   .... (able)

16. defens........   .... (ible)

17. inexor........   .... (able)

18. comprehens..,...... .... (ible)

19. collect........ .... (ible)

20. present........ .... (able)

21. replace........ .... (able)

22. communic........ .... (able)

23. access........ .... (ible)

24. hospit........ .... (able)

25. irrepress........ .... (ible)

26. convert........ .... (ible)

27. inevit........ .... (able)

28. irresist........ .... (ible)

29. contempt........ .... (ible)

30. collaps........ .... (ible)

II. Each word below is deliberately misspelled (or is in its less preferable form). Cross it out and rewrite it correctly.

1. relidgious .:............................... (religious)

2. sacriledge .... (sacrilege)

3. sacreligious .... (sacrilegious)

4. priviledge .... (privilege)

5. pidgeon .... (pigeon)

6. occassional .... (occasional)

7. passtime .... (pastime)

8. tresspass .... (trespass)

9. obeissance .... (obeisance)

10. dumbfound .... (dumfound)

11. numbskull   .... (numskull)

12. succomb   .... (succumb)

13. agressive   .... (aggressive)

14. aggree   .... (agree)

15. dissagree   .... (disagree)

16. supress   .... (suppress)

17. suport   .... (support)

18. supose   .... (suppose)

III. Check the word that correctly completes each statement.

1. A rule or truth is a (a) principal,
   (b) principle.   (b)
2. Money on which interest is paid is one's
   (a) principle, (b) principal.   (b)
3. The adjective meaning *main* is spelled
   (a) principal, (b) principle.   (a)
4. Writing materials are called
   (a) stationery, (b) stationary.   (a)
5. (a) Stationery, (b) Stationary means
   fixed, not movable.   (b)
6. A musical sound may be made up of
   (a) cords, (b) chords.   (b)
7. Human sounds are produced through
   the vocal (a) cords, (b) chords.   (a)
8. To (a) pour, (b) pore over material
   is to study it carefully.   (b)
9. Some skirts are (a) flaired, (b) flared.   (b)
10. To pretend is to (a) faint, (b) feint.   (b)
11. A big gun is a (a) cannon, (b) canon.   (a)
12. Before *breath* the correct word is
    (a) bated, (b) baited.   (a)
13. A barren region is a (a) dessert,
    (b) desert.   (b)

14. To solicit door to door is to
   (a) canvass, (b) canvas.   (a)

IV. Check the correct spelling of each word.

1. (a) business, (b) buisness   (a)
2. (a) amoung, (b) among   (b)
3. (a) disheveled, (b) dissheveled   (a)
4. (a) threshold, (b) threshhold   (a)
5. (a) withold, (b) withhold   (b)
6. (a) fourty, (b) forty   (b)
7. (a) grateful, (b) greatful   (a)
8. (a) hairbrained, (b) harebrained   (b)
9. (a) kimono, (b) kimona   (a)
10. (a) kakhi, (b) khaki   (b)
11. (a) nickle, (b) nickel   (b)
12. (a) mineralogy, (b) minerology   (a)
13. (a) straight jacket, (b) strait jacket   (b)
14. (a) yeoman, (b) yoeman   (a)
15. (a) sodder, (b) solder   (b)
16. (a) vittles, (b) victuals   (b)
17. (a) rythm, (b) rhythm   (b)
18. (a) paraffin, (b) parrafin   (a)
19. (a) genealogy, (b) geneology   (a)
20. (a) prespiration, (b) perspiration   (b)
21. (a) prescription, (b) perscription   (a)
22. (a) protuberant, (b) protruberant   (a)
23. (a) smoothe, (b) smooth   (b)
24. (a) repetition, (b) repitition   (a)
25. (a) manafacture, (b) manufacture   (b)

V. Answer the following questions by writing -ABLE or -IBLE.

1. If the root is a full word, the ending is likely

   to be ....   (able)

2. If the root is not a full word, the ending is

   likely to be ....   (ible)

3. After a "soft" G, the ending is .... (ible)

4. If the root is a full word lacking only final E,
   the ending is .... (able)

5. After a "soft" C, the ending is .... (ible)

6. If the root ends in MISS-, the ending
   is .... (ible)

7. After a "hard" G, the ending is .... (able)

8. If the root ends in -NS, the ending is
   usually .... (ible)

9. After a "hard" C, the ending is .... (able)

10. If the root is followed by A in some other
    form of the word, use......... (able)

11. After I, the ending is .... (able)

12. If -ION immediately follows the root in
    a related word, the ending is usually .... (ible)

Chapter 33.

MORE ON "MULTIPLE REPRESENTATION"

We know, by now, that "multiple representation" is one of the prime causes, perhaps *the* prime cause, for most people's difficulties with English spelling.

For example, GHOTI might be a reasonable spelling for the word which we normally write as FISH.

For GH sometimes has the sound of F, as in ENOUGH.

And O sometimes has the sound of short I, as in WOMEN.

And TI often has the sound of SH, as in NATION, INHIBITION, etc.

Everyone, of course, can spell FISH, and would never, with any sanity, dream of spelling it GHOTI.

But many of us do get confused when we have to make a choice between C, S, and SC.

The same consonant sound, for example, is represented in COMPETENCE by -CE, in LICENSE by -SE, in CONVALESCE by -SCE, and in REGRESS by -SS.

Or, again, the same sound (SH) is represented in SUGAR by S, in CAPRICIOUS by CI, in LUSCIOUS by SCI, in PASSION by SSI, in FASHION by SHI, and in PATIENT by TI.

Is it any wonder, then, that even the most literate of us have to check every now and then on the correct patterns of words we've used all our lives? Or that we misspell common words without the slightest awareness of error?

Today we shall learn to avoid both confusion and unconscious error by mastering all the commonly misspelled words in which there is a reasonable choice between C, S, and SC.

I. -ENSE or -ENCE?

There are, as I have pointed out in the past, a number of broad and reliable principles that govern English spelling. We can note, as an instance, that verbs ending in -ND generally have derivative forms in which the D changes to S.

Consider:

> compreheND—compreheNSible
> appreheND—appreheNSion
> expaND—expaNSe
> expeND—expeNSe
> repreheND—repreheNSible

It stands to reason, then (which is not to suggest that *all* spellings are reasonable!), that the verbs DEFEND, OFFEND, PRETEND, and SUSPEND will have related forms in which the D become S. And so they do.

> defeND—defeNSe
> offeND—offeNSe
> preteND—preteNSe
> suspeND—suspeNSe

Our British cousins, as it happens, prefer the patterns DEFENCE, OFFENCE, and PRETENCE, but the American spellings are as indicated above. Nevertheless, many Americans blithely write -ENCE in the four words under consideration. And they can hardly be blamed, since so many words do end this way—COMPETENCE, VIOLENCE, NEGLIGENCE, EVIDENCE, and hundreds more. These -ENCE forms, however, all come from adjectives ending in -ENT (COMPETENT, VIOLENT, NEGLIGENT, EVIDENT), not from verbs in -ND. And it is understandable that people's fondness for the -ENCE ending tempts them into misspelling LICENSE and INCENSE as LICENCE and INCENCE.

So let us be particularly careful of these six -ENSE words. Study the underlined areas carefully, then cover and rewrite.

1. DEF<u>ENSE</u>   ....

2. OFF<u>ENSE</u>   ....

3. PRET<u>ENSE</u>   ....

4. SUSP<u>ENSE</u>   ....

5. LIC<u>ENSE</u>   ....

6. INC<u>ENSE</u>   ....

II. In words like GRACIOUS, CAPRICIOUS, AUDA-
CIOUS, etc., the sound SH is represented by CI. One is not
surprised, then, that in the following words a poor speller
is tempted to use the same CI pattern for the same sound.
However, since these words come from the Latin verb *scio*,
to know, the S may not be omitted. Practice them:

7. CON<u>SCI</u>ENCE   ....

8. CON<u>SCI</u>OUS   ....

9. UNCON<u>SCI</u>OUS   ....

10. OMNI<u>SCI</u>ENCE   ....

III. The SC combination is important also in the following:

11. AB<u>SC</u>ESS   ....

12. LU<u>SC</u>IOUS   ....

13. LA<u>SC</u>IVIOUS   ....

14. VI<u>SC</u>ERA   ....

15. RESU<u>SC</u>ITATE   ....

16. IRIDE<u>SC</u>ENT   ....

17. ADOLE<u>SC</u>ENT   ....

18. CONVALE<u>SC</u>ENT   ....

IV. With SC such a common pattern, we must be careful of two words in which only an S or a C is used, *not* both.

19. AB<u>S</u>ENCE ....

From the adjective ABSENT, which has no C; not *abscence*.

20. VI<u>C</u>IOUS ....

From VICE, which has no S; not *viscious*.

These are words whose correct patterns are easy to remember once you've concentrated on them. It is not even particularly dangerous to let you see the common misspellings. So cross out every incorrect pattern below and rewrite the word correctly.

1. defence

.... (DEFENSE)

2. offence

.... (OFFENSE)

3. pretence

.... (PRETENSE)

4. suspence

.... (SUSPENSE)

5. liscence

.... (LICENSE)

6. incence

.... (INCENSE)

7. concience

.... (CONSCIENCE)

8. concious

    .... (CONSCIOUS)

9. unconcious

    .... (UNCONSCIOUS)

10. omnicience

    .... (OMNISCIENCE)

11. absess

    .... (ABSCESS)

12. lushious

    .... (LUSCIOUS)

13. lacivious

    .... (LASCIVIOUS)

14. visera

    .... (VISCERA)

15. resusitate

    .... (RESUSCITATE)

16. iridesent

    .... (IRIDESCENT)

17. adolesent

    .... (ADOLESCENT)

18. convalesent

    .... (CONVALESCENT)

19. abscence

    .... (ABSENCE)

20. viscious

....   (VICIOUS)

Now, finally, to make mastery doubly certain, fill in the
missing letters, then rewrite each word.

1. AB__ESS .   ... (SC)

2. PRETEN_E   .... (S)

3. VI__ERA   .... (SC)

4. VL_IOUS   .... (C)

5. CON__IOUS   .... (SC)

6. IRIDE__ENT   .... (SC)

7. DEFEN_E   .... (S)

8. UNCON__IOUS   .... (SC)

9. ADOLE__ENT   .... (SC)

10. INCEN_E   .... (S)

11. AB_ENCE   .... (S)

12. LU__IOUS   .... (SC)

13. CONVALE__ENT   .... (SC)

14. SUSPEN_E   .... (S)

15. LL_EN_E   .... (C, S)

16. OMNI__IENCE   .... (SC)

17. OFFEN_E   .... (S)

18. CON__IENCE   .... (SC)

19. RESU__ITATE   .... (SC)

20. LA__IVIOUS   .... (SC)

Teaser Preview of Tomorrow's Chapter

Which is the commoner ending for verbs: -CEDE or
-CEED? Can you think of examples that use one or the
other? How about -IFY or -EFY? Can you again think of
examples?

Write your answers below:

1. -CEDE

....

....

2. -CEED

....

....

3. -IFY

....

....

4. -EFY

....

....

Chapter 34.

THREE SPECIAL PITFALLS FOR THE UNWARY

Words can most efficiently and most successfully be learned in groups which have a unifying principle, since there is some meaningful relation that can be observed and remembered.

Take the verbs that end in the sound *-seed*. Some are spelled -CEDE, a few -CEED, and one lone nonconformist ends in -SEDE. (Can you think of the only -SEDE verb in the language?)

I. Seven common verbs (and, of course, CEDE itself) end in -CEDE. Study each one, then cover it and rewrite.

1. ACCEDE ....

2. PRECEDE ....

3. CONCEDE ....

4. RECEDE ....

5. SECEDE ....

6. INTERCEDE ....

7. ANTECEDE ....

II. Three, *and only three*, verbs end in -CEED. These merit special study.

8. SUCCEED ....

9. PROCEED ....

10. EXCEED ....

Bear in mind that PRO<u>CEED</u> is a -CEED verb; PRE-<u>CEDE</u> is a -CEDE verb. And note that the noun PRO-<u>CED</u>URE has only one E following the C.

III. One, *and only one,* verb ends in -SEDE—indeed, this is the only word in the language with this uncommon ending.

11. SUPERSEDE ....
SUPERSEDE is a combination of two Latin roots—
super, above, and *sed-,* sit—if one thing SUPERSEDES another, it etymologically *sits above* it, and thus pushes it out and takes its place. The root *sed-* is found also in SEDENTARY, involved with sitting, as a SEDEN-TARY occupation, and SEDIMENT, matter that falls to and sits at the bottom.

Ready for some practice? Put the correct ending on each verb (or in the case of number 7, fill in the missing letter or letters), then rewrite the complete word.

1. AC_____ .... (CEDE)

2. SUPER_____ .... (SEDE)

3. RE_____ .... (CEDE)

4. SUC_____ .... (CEED)

5. ANTE_____ .... (CEDE)

6. SE_____ .... (CEDE)

7. PROC_DURE .... (E)

8. PRO_____ .... (CEED)

9. CON_____ .... (CEDE)

10. EX_____ .... (CEED)

11. INTER_____ .... (CEDE)

12. PRE_____ .... (CEDE)

IV. It is not difficult to think of verbs ending in -IFY. TESTIFY, PACIFY, INTENSIFY, VERIFY, CERTIFY, and scores of others spring readily to mind. These, and hundreds like them, present no problem.

But four—and only four—common verbs end in -EFY. It is only natural that these four are misspelled -IFY by the most educated, not excluding teachers of English in high school and college.

I ask you to commit these four conspicuous exceptions to memory—and as a help to that end I offer you the word PEARLS, each of the consonants of which is the initial letter of one of the words.

1. P stands for PUTREFY, to make or become rotten or putrid, to decompose. Meat PUTREFIES if not refrigerated.

   Write the word: ....

2. R stands for RAREFY, to make or become thin, less dense, or purer. The higher the altitude the more RAREFIED the atmosphere. The word is also used figuratively—he was uncomfortable in the RAREFIED atmosphere of college faculty meetings.

   Write the word: ....

3. L stands for LIQUEFY, to make or become liquid. Metals LIQUEFY at very high temperatures.

   Write the word: ....

4. And S stands for STUPEFY, to render dull or make stuporous, to astonish or amaze. He was STUPEFIED when he heard the news.

   Write the word: ....

Derived forms are correspondingly spelled—PUTREFACTION, RAREFACTION, LIQUEFACTION, STUPEFACTION.

(It is an odd thing—and oddities, as you know, abound in English spelling—that the adjectives that are related to three of these verbs, namely PUTR**I**D, LIQU**I**D, and STUP**I**D, contain an I in the very place where the verb has an E.)

Examine these verbs and their derived forms once again, noting particularly the crucial E, then rewrite.

1. PUTR**E**FY ....

2. RAR**E**FY ....

3. LIQU**E**FY ....

4. STUP**E**FY ....

5. PUTR**E**FACTION ....

6. RAR**E**FACTION ....

7. LIQU**E**FACTION ....

8. STUP**E**FACTION ....

9. PUTR**E**FIED ....

10. RAR**E**FIED ....

11. LIQU**E**FIED ....

12. STUP**E**FIED ....

13. PUTR**E**FYING ....

14. RAR**E**FYING ....

15. LIQU**E**FYING ....

16. STUP**E**FYING ....

V. You know that more verbs end in -IZE than in -ISE. Did you know that *only two* common verbs end in -YZE? These are ANAL**YZE** and PARAL**YZE**. (A few technical terms, such as ELECTROL**YZE** and CATAL**YZE** also belong to this group, but anyone using them is likely to spell them correctly.)

All derived forms of these two will also have a Y directly after the L. Examine and rewrite the following:

1. ANAL<u>YZE</u> ....

2. PSYCHOANAL<u>YZE</u> ....

3. ANAL<u>Y</u>ST ....

4. PSYCHOANAL<u>Y</u>ST ....

5. ANAL<u>Y</u>TIC ....

6. PSYCHOANAL<u>Y</u>TIC ....

7. ANAL<u>Y</u>SIS ....

8. PSYCHOANAL<u>Y</u>SIS ....

9. PARAL<u>YZE</u> ....

10. PARAL<u>Y</u>TIC ....

11. PARAL<u>Y</u>SIS ....

VI. So . . .

-CEDE is the commoner ending but we must take care with EX<u>CEED</u>, PRO<u>CEED</u>, SUC<u>CEED</u>, and SUPER-<u>SEDE</u>.

-IFY is the almost universal ending, but we must be on guard with PUTR<u>EFY</u>, RAR<u>EFY</u>, LIQU<u>EFY</u>, and STUP<u>EFY</u>.

-IZE is the common ending, but we must watch out for ANAL<u>YZE</u> and PARAL<u>YZE</u>.

Similarly, -CY is more frequently found than -SY as a terminal syllable (LEGACY, LUNACY, LITERACY, INFANCY, etc.). So, as you would suspect, many people write -CY where -SY is required, usually without the slightest hesitation or doubt. As, for example, in these demons:

1. ECST<u>ASY</u> ....

2. HYPOCRI<u>SY</u> ....

3. HER<u>ESY</u> ....

4. IDIOSYNCRASY   ....

5. APOSTASY   ....

Note that the vowel preceding the -SY is also often subject to error. Derived forms of these nouns are easier to spell, since the crucial vowel is more clearly pronounced: ECSTATIC, HYPOCRITICAL and HYPOCRITE, HERETICAL, IDIOSYNCRATIC, APOSTATE. A few spellers have trouble also with the first Y in HYPOCRISY and IDIOSYNCRASY.

Ready for some more practice? Fill in the missing letters then rewrite the complete word.

1. MAGN_FY   .... (I)

2. CLASS_FY   .... (I)

3. RAR_FY   .... (E)

4. PUTR_FY   .... (E)

5. PUR_FY   .... (I)

6. LIQU_FY   .... (E)

7. MOD_FY   .... (I)

8. STUP_FY   .... (E)

9. IDENT_FY   .... (I)

10. PUTR_FACTION   .... (E)

11. RAR_FACTION   .... (E)

12. LIQU_FACTION   .... (E)

13. STUP_FACTION   .... (E)

14. SIMPL_FIED   .... (I)

15. ORGAN_ZE   .... (I)

16. PARAL_ZE   .... (Y)

17. IMMUN_ZE .... (I)

18. PSYCHOANAL_ZE .... (Y)

19. ANAL_S_S .... (Y, I)

20. PARAL_S_S .... (Y, I)

21. PARAL_TIC .... (Y)

22. ANAL_TIC .... (Y)

23. ANAL_ST .... (Y)

24. ECSTA_Y .... (S)

25. APOST__Y .... (AS)

26. H_POCR__Y .... (Y, IS)

27. IDIOS_NCR__Y .... (Y, AS)

28. HER__Y .... (ES)

Teaser Preview for Tomorrow

If PANIC is spelled as indicated, why is *panicy* a misspelling?

Chapter 35.

KEEPING C "HARD"

You will recall that C is generally pronounced "soft" (i.e., like S) before the vowel E, as in ENFORCE, CENT, CELL, etc.

E, however, is not the only vowel that makes a C "soft"; so does the vowel I, as in TENACITY, CISTERN, CIVILIZE, etc.; and so does Y (Y is a vowel when it has the sound of I, as in RHYTHM, or PRY, or of long E, as in WORTHY), as in CYST, CYNOSURE, or ICY.

On the other hand, C is always "hard" (i.e., like K) at the end of a word—PANIC, FROLIC, TRAFFIC, etc.

To repeat, then . . .

C is "soft" before E, I, and Y.

C is "hard" as a final letter.

Suppose, now, we wish to add -Y to the word PANIC . . .

Or -ER to the word PICNIC . . .

Or -ING to the word FROLIC . . .

Then we're in trouble, aren't we?

Because the "hard" C of PANIC, PICNIC, and FROLIC becomes, by rule, "soft" before E, I, and Y.

And that throws the pronunciation off.

What do we do, in such cases?

The only thing possible—we insert a K between the C and the softening vowel.

Getting PANICKY, PICNICKER, and FROLICKING —and preserving the "hard" sound of C.

Let's examine all the common words ending in C in which a K must be inserted before -ER, -ED, -ING, or -Y. Study each one, understand the reason for the very necessary K, then rewrite.

1. PANICKY ....

2. PANICKED ....

3. PANICKING ....

4. PICNICKED ....

5. PICNICKER ....

6. PICNICKING ....

7. FROLICKED ....

8. FROLICKER ....

9. FROLICKING ....

10. TRAFFICKED ....

11. TRAFFICKER ....

12. TRAFFICKING ....

13. MIMICKED ....

14. COLICKY ....

15. MIMICKING ....

16. PHYSICKED ....

17. POLITICKING ....

18. SHELLACKED ....

19. SHELLACKING ....

20. BIVOUACKED ....

21. ZINCKY ....

(In FROLICSOME, of course, no K is necessary. Why
not?)

Preview Teaser for Tomorrow

Is there any way to be sure whether to use a single C or a
double C?

Chapter 36.

MORE ON TRICKY DOUBLE CONSONANTS

As we have learned, a double consonant usually has the same sound as a single consonant. INOCULATE has one N and one C, INNOCUOUS has double N and one C, yet the sound of the first two syllables is the same in both words. VACUUM has one C, RACCOON has two—yet the sound of C is the same in both.

Most often (but this is by no means universal enough for us to get a hard and fast rule out of it), a double, rather than a single, consonant closes the accented syllable of a word, in which case the preceding vowel is short—that is, A as in HAT, E as in BET, I as in BIT, O as in HOT, or U as in BUT.

Examples of this tendency are words like MATTER, BETTER, BITTER, HOTTER, and BUTTER, in all of which the accent is on the first syllable and the vowel preceding the double T is short. Other and similar examples: ACCURATE, MESSAGE, PILLOW, SORROW, SLUGGISH—all the double consonants closing the accented syllable, each vowel in that syllable short.

Indeed, it is this very common tendency which seduces people into misspelling words like RECOMMEND, VACUUM, DESICCATE, and INOCULATE, in which, contrarily, a *single* consonant closes an accented syllable containing a short vowel.

Consider, now, some words that follow the common tendency we have mentioned, but that some people nevertheless often misspell. Note that the underlined syllable is accented, contains a short vowel, and ends with a double consonant.

1. <u>BROCCOLI</u> ....
   (A kind of vegetable.)

2. IMPE<u>CC</u>ABLE ....
   (Faultless; without error or blemish.)

3. MORO<u>CC</u>O ....
   (A kind of leather.)

4. <u>MO</u>CCASIN ....
   (A kind of slipper or soft shoe.)

5. PI<u>CC</u>OLO ....
   (A musical instrument.)

6. TOBA<u>CC</u>O ....

7. BU<u>CC</u>ANEER ....
   (A pirate.)

8. PI<u>CC</u>ALILLI ....
   (A kind of relish. There are two accents in this word,
   one on the first, one on the third syllable—both end
   with a double consonant.)

9. <u>MEZZ</u>ANINE ....
   (A balcony or gallery—the final syllable is also accented but does not contain a short vowel.)

10. <u>QUIZZES</u> ....

11. SA<u>BB</u>ATH ....

12. ACCO<u>MM</u>ODATE ....
    (The C is also doubled—we'll deal with that problem
    in a later chapter.)

13. COM<u>MITT</u>EE ....
    (Note, also, the double M.)

14. <u>CINN</u>AMON ....
    (A spice.)

15. RE<u>CONN</u>AISSANCE ....
    (Obtaining of information about an enemy area—note,
    also, the double S.)

16. MILLE**NN**IUM   ....
    (Note also the double L.)

Please bear in mind that there are many words which run
counter to this principle, most of them, as a result, generally misspelled. Some of these have already been covered in
past chapters—others will be discussed later on.

For the moment, let us concentrate on the 16 demons we
are dealing with today. Supply the missing letter or letters
in each one below, then rewrite the complete word.

1. BRO__OLI	....	(CC)
2. TOBA__O	....	(CC)
3. SA__ATH	....	(BB)
4. ME__ANINE	....	(ZZ)
5. BU__ANEER	....	(CC)
6. MO__ASIN	....	(CC)
7. MILLE__IUM	....	(NN)
8. RECO__AISSANCE	....	(NN)
9. QUI__ES	....	(ZZ)
10. PI__ALILLI	....	(CC)
11. IMPE__ABLE	....	(CC)
12. CI__AMON	....	(NN)
13. ACCO__ODATE	....	(MM)
14. MORO__O	....	(CC)
15. COMMI__EE	....	(TT)
16. PI__OLO	....	(CC)

Try some of the same words again, filling in different letters this time, and again rewriting the complete word.

1. PICCO_O   .... (L)
2. A__OMMODATE   .... (CC)
3. RECONNAI__ANCE   .... (SS)
4. BROCCO_I   .... (L)
5. PICCA_ILLI   .... (L)
6. PICCALI__I   .... (LL)
7. BUCCA_EER   .... (N)
8. MO__OCCO   .... (R)
9. CINN__MON   .... (A)
10. CO__ITTEE   .... (MM)
11. MI__ENNIUM   .... (LL)
12. MOCCA__IN   .... (S)

Can you finally write the word that fits each definition?

1. A musical instrument

   (P-)   .... (PICCOLO)

2. A kind of vegetable

   (B-)   .... (BROCCOLI)

3. A component of cigars and
   cigarettes

   (T-)   .... (TOBACCO)

4. A pirate

   (B-)   .... (BUCCANEER)

5. Military observation

   (R-)   .... (RECONNAISSANCE)

6. The plural of QUIZ

   (QU-) ....(QUIZZES)

7. Period of peace, happiness, etc.,
   expected in the future

   (M-)   ....(MILLENNIUM)

8. Group assigned to a specific
   task

   (C-)   ....(COMMITTEE)

9. Sunday; holy day

   (S-)   ....(SABBATH)

10. Faultless

   (I-)   ....(IMPECCABLE)

11. A kind of leather

   (M-)   ....(MOROCCO)

12. A spice

   (C-)   ....(CINNAMON)

13. Give lodging or space to

   (A-)   ....(ACCOMMODATE)

14. A kind of relish

   (P-)   ....(PICCALILLI)

15. Gallery

   (M-)   ....(MEZZANINE)

16. A slipper

   (M-)   ....(MOCCASIN)

Chapter 37

AND NOW TRICKY SINGLE CONSONANTS

But there are words, as I have warned you, in which either a *single* consonant closes an accented syllable, or a double consonant closes an *unaccented* syllable—contrary to, and in sheer defiance of, the general tendency.

Many of these you have already mastered in earlier chapters—14 important, and frequently misspelled, rebels and nonconformists are our concern today.

I. Note that in the following words the underlined syllable is *accented*, but ends nonetheless in a *single* consonant.

1. CORR<u>O</u>BORATE   ....

   On the contrary, the first syllable, unaccented, ends in double R.

2. <u>HAR</u>ASS   ....

   The more scholarly pronunciation accents the *first* syllable; if, like many others, you accent the *last* syllable, you should find no spelling problem in this word. Say it as you prefer, but write it with only one R.

3. <u>REC</u>ONNOITER   ....

   Only one C, though the accent falls on the first syllable. It's the N that's doubled, as in RE<u>CONN</u>AISSANCE, which comes from the same French root.

4. IMM<u>AC</u>ULATE   ....

   The accented syllable ends in a single C; the unaccented first syllable contrarily ends in a double M.

5. <u>MAC</u>AROON   ....

One C, one R.

6. <u>MAC</u>ARONI   ....

Again one C, one R.

7. <u>HAZ</u>ARD   ....

One Z.

II. Note that in the following words the underlined syllable
is *unaccented,* but ends nonetheless in a *double* consonant.

8. MAY<u>ONN</u>AISE   ....

Of the three syllables, the middle one receives no accent at all—it is nevertheless closed with a double N.

9. <u>RACC</u>OON   ....

Again, an unaccented syllable ends in a double consonant. RACOON is technically also correct, but not
popular.

10. <u>CONN</u>OISSEUR   ....

The primary accent falls on the last syllable, but a
double N closes the first one. The three words REC-
<u>ONN</u>OITER, REC<u>ONN</u>AISSANCE, and <u>CONN</u>OIS-
SEUR all come from forms of the French verb *con-
naître,* to know; the CONN- combination is unalter-
able no matter where the accent falls in English.

11. <u>TOCC</u>ATA   ....

12. <u>PIZZ</u>ICATO   ....

13. <u>STACC</u>ATO   ....

14. O<u>BBL</u>IGATO   ....

In these four musical terms, the primary accent is on

the next-to-the-last syllable (the words are pronounced to-KAH-ta, pit-zee-KAH-to, sta-KAH-to, ob-li-GAH-to), but the double consonant closes the first syllable. (A variant spelling, OBLIGATO, is also technically correct, but not recommended.)

Is your visual memory becoming trained to react affirmatively only to the correct combination in the 30 words of this and the preceding chapter? Are your fingers becoming accustomed to doubling the proper consonant in each one? Let us put it to a further test—supply the missing letter or letters, then rewrite the complete word.

1. CORRO_ORATE   .... (B)

2. HA_ASS   .... (R)

3. RE_ONNOITER   .... (C)

4. IMMA_ULATE   .... (C)

5. MA_AROON   .... (C)

6. MA_ARONI   .... (C)

7. HA_ARD   .... (Z)

8. MAYO_AISE   .... (NN)

9. RA_OON   .... (CC)

10. CO_OISSEUR   .... (NN)

11. TO_ATA   .... (CC)

12. PI_ICATO   .... (ZZ)

13. STA_ATO   .... (CC)

14. O_LIGATO   .... (BB)

15. CO_OBORATE   .... (RR)

16. RECO_OITER   .... (NN)

17. I_ACULATE   .... (MM)

18. CONNOI_EUR   .... (SS)

19. TOCCA_A   .... (T)

20. PIZZICA_O   .... (T)

21. STACCA_O   .... (T)

22. OBBLIGA_O   .... (T)

23. BRO__OLI   .... (CC)

24. IMPE__ABLE   .... (CC)

25. MORO__O   .... (CC)

26. MO__ASIN   .... (CC)

27. PI__OLO   .... (CC)

28. TOBA__O   .... (CC)

29. BU__ANEER   .... (CC)

30. PI__ALILLI   .... (CC)

31. ME__ANINE   .... (ZZ)

32. QUI__ES   .... (ZZ)

33. SA__ATH   .... (BB)

34. ACCO__ODATE   .... (MM)

35. COMMI__EE   .... (TT)

36. CI__AMON   .... (NN)

37. RECO__AISSANCE .... (NN)

38. MILLE__IUM   .... (NN)

39. MO_OCCO   .... (R)

40. MOCCA_IN   .... (S)

41. PICCALL_I   .... (LL)

42. A__OMMODATE   .... (CC)

43. CO__ITTEE   .... (MM)

44. CINNAM_N   .... (O)

45. RE_ONNAISSANCE   .... (C)

46. MI__ENNIUM   .... (LL)

47. PICCA_ILLI   .... (L)

Chapter 38.

DOUBLING C, G, AND L

In a selected list of 25 words, the problem is whether or not to double the C, G, or L after initial A in the first syllable. These can best be mastered by training your visual and muscular memory.

I. *Note the double C.*

1. A**CC**UMULATE ....

2. A**CC**RUE ....

3. A**CC**OST ....

4. A**CC**ORDI**O**N ....
   (Note also the O in the final syllable.)

5. A**CC**OMPLISH ....

6. A**CC**O**MM**ODATE ....
   (Note, also, the double M.)

7. A**CC**LAIM ....

Two others have only one C following the initial A; but in these, perversely, the poor speller, accustomed to writing ACC-, often slips in an unwarranted extra C. Watch the following:

8. A**C**OUSTICS ....

9. A**C**ROSS ....

II. *Note the double G.*

10. AGGRAVATE ....

11. AGGREGATE ....

12. AGGRIEVED ....

13. AGGRESSIVE ....

But only one G in:

14. AGREE ....

15. DISAGREE ....

16. AGREEABLE ....

17. DISAGREEABLE ....

18. AGREEMENT ....

19. DISAGREEMENT ....

III. *Note the double L.*

20. ALLEGE ....

21. ALLEGIANCE ....

22. ALLEGRO ....

23. ALLOT ....

24. ALLUDE ....

25. ALLURE ....

Test Your Learning

I. Fill in the missing letter or letters, then rewrite the complete word.

1. DISA_REE .... (G)

2. A_OUSTICS .... (C)

3. A__UMULATE .... (CC)

4. A_REEABLE .... (G)

5. A__EGE .... (LL)

6. A__OT .... (LL)

7. A__RUE .... (CC)

8. A__RESSIVE .... (GG)

9. A__REGATE .... (GG)

10. A_REE .... (G)

11. A__ORDION .... (CC)

12. A__OMMODATE .... (CC)

13. A__EGIANCE .... (LL)

14. A_ROSS .... (C)

15. A__OST .... (CC)

16. A__OMPLISH .... (CC)

17. A__LAIM .... (CC)

18. A__RAVATE .... (GG)

19. DISA_REE .... (G)

20. A__RIEVED .... (GG)

21. A_REEMENT .... (G)

22. DISA_REEMENT .... (G)

23. A__EGRO .... (LL)

24. A__URE .... (LL)

25. A__UDE .... (LL)

26. ACCORDI_N .... (O)

27. ACCO__ODATE .... (MM)

28. DI_AGREE   .... (S)
29. DI_AGREEMENT   .... (S)
30. ALLE_E   .... (G)
31. AGGR__VED   .... (IE)

II. Of the following 17 words, exactly ten are misspelled.
If a pattern is correct, check the space; if incorrect, rewrite
it correctly.

1. acrue

....   (ACCRUE)

2. accross

....   (ACROSS)

3. accoustics

....   (ACOUSTICS)

4. accost

....   (∨)

5. acclaim

....   (∨)

6. accordian

....   (ACCORDION)

7. agressive

....   (AGGRESSIVE)

8. allegro

....   (∨)

9. aggrieved

....   (∨)

10. dissagree

....   (DISAGREE)

11. aggravate

....   (√)

12. aggregate

....   (√)

13. alledge

....   (ALLEGE)

14. allude

....   (√)

15. alotted

....   (ALLOTTED)

16. acommodate

....   (ACCOMMODATE)

17. accomodate

....   (ACCOMMODATE)

Chapter 39.

THIRTY SUPER-DEMONS

Expert violinists, pianists, surgeons, and typists seem to think with their fingers; or, to use a different image, their fingers appear to have an existence of their own, as they fly through the most complicated tasks with split-second efficiency and perfect accuracy.

Such skill comes only from careful training and years of unceasing practice.

Training and practice are equally necessary in the making of the expert speller—training that stores up in the visual memory a vast reservoir of correct patterns, sufficient practice to enable the fingers to reproduce these patterns quickly and correctly without conscious guidance fom the mind.

These chapters help you to build up, day by day, a keen visual memory that accepts only the proper patterns of commonly misspelled words and rejects any deviation, no matter how slight. And the repeated practice in writing these words, offered on almost every page, will eventually develop in you such fine co-ordination between brain and fingers that complete accuracy in spelling will occur almost automatically. *With enough intelligent practice, you will never have to think how to spell a word—you will simply spell it with complete confidence that you are absolutely right.*

So as we go through these demons group by group, conscientiously do every exercise, linger fondly over every underlined letter or combination of letters, write each complete word as often as required, and check every response immediately in order to reinforce your learning and root out any proneness to error.

Keep these important instructions in mind as you work on today's words. Every one of them is certain to be misspelled by the untutored; many of them send even the most literate of people thumbing through the dictionary. And in each word one special area, underlined and explained, causes most if not all the trouble. Study the letters underlined, read the explanation, then immediately cover the word and see whether you can write it correctly.

1. OPPRESS
   Resist the impulse to use a single P, despite the one P in DEPRESS and REPRESS. OPPRESS is formed from the Latin prefix *ob-* plus the root *-press*, and the combination of B and P becomes a double P.

   Write the word: ....

2. PLEBEIAN (ordinary, commonplace, unimaginative)
   Watch that I—most people carelessly leave it out.

   Write the word: ....

3. CURVACEOUS (full of curves—said of women's figures)
   Most similar-sounding words end in -ACIOUS (TENACIOUS, AUDACIOUS, etc.)—this one ends in -ACEOUS.

   Write the word: ....

4. SAPPHIRE (a gem)
   For pronunciation one P may be enough, but PP is required in spelling.

   Write the word: ....

5. WALNUT
   Great temptation to double the L; *don't*.

   Write the word: ....

6. WELFARE
   Same temptation; same restriction.

   Write the word: ....

7. WELCOME
Again, as in WALNUT and WELFARE, logic dictates an incorrect double L—be illogical and spell it right.

Write the word: ....

8. PRESUMPTUOUS (presuming; taking too much for granted)
Because the underlined portion is so often gaily ignored in pronunciation, it is often similarly slighted in spelling. To be correct, both say and write the crucial letters.

Write the word: ....

9. CHAGRINED (disappointed, embarrassed)
The startling single N in this word was mentioned in passing in chapter 11, but it's worth thinking about again.

Write the word: ....

10. KIDNAPED
This word, too, was brought to your attention in chapter 11, when it was pointed out that a single P was the preferable pattern here and also in KIDNAPER and KIDNAPING.

Write the word: ....

11. APOCRYPHAL (of doubtful authenticity)
You'd be amazed how many educated people think there is an H after the C—as you can see, R follows directly.

Write the word: ....

12. SYCOPHANT (a bootlicker; a "yes man")
Here, too, many writers sense the need for an H following C—a totally illusory need, as it happens.

Write the word: ....

13. CHRYSANTHEMUM (a flower)
Here an H does follow C, and, perversely, some people
leave it out. The rest of the word is spelled exactly as
pronounced.

Write the word: ....

14. MACABRE (gruesome, horrible)
It is hard to understand why some writers, overgener-
ous, like to spell this word with two C's, but they do,
just as they use, incorrectly, a double S in OCCA-
SIONAL. This is one of the very few words in American spelling (ACRE is another) that ends in -RE rather
than -ER.

Write the word: ....

15. MARVELOUS
Like all other derivatives of the verb MARVEL (MAR-
VELED, MARVELING, etc.), this adjective preferably has only one L. It's all a matter of accent, as you
recall from chapters 10 and 11.

Write the word: ....

A Pause for Practice

Each one of the 15 demons we've examined so far has one
stumbling block, one crucial area where poor or inexpert
spellers generally go astray. You know where that is, now,
and how to get through it safely. So, to continue training
your fingers, fill in the missing letter or letters, then rewrite
the complete word.

1. KIDNA_ED   .... (P)

2. WE_FARE   .... (L)

3. CHAGRI_ED   .... (N)

4. PLEB__AN   .... (EI)

5. SA__HIRE   .... (PP)

6. MARVE_OUS .... (L)

7. C___SANTHEMUM .... (HRY)

8. WE_COME .... (L)

9. APOC__PHAL .... (RY)

10. MA_ABRE .... (C)

11. O__RESS .... (PP)

12. SYC_PHANT .... (O)

13. WA_NUT .... (L)

14. CURVAC_OUS .... (E)

15. PRESUM__OUS .... (PTU)

Let's try some more.

16. STIMULUS (incentive, spur)
Because so many *adjectives* end in -OUS, careless spellers put the same ending on this *noun*. But there's no O in the word.

Write the word: ....

17. ESOPHAGUS (gullet; passage from the pharynx to the stomach)
The same error is usually made here as in the preceding word—again a *noun,* so the adjectival ending -OUS cannot be used. (Nouns end in -US: STIMULUS, ESOPHAGUS, SARCOPHAGUS, CALCULUS, CALLUS, IMPETUS, OEDIPUS, INCUBUS, SUCCUBUS, HIPPOPOTAMUS, etc.; adjectives end in -OUS: DEVIOUS, WONDROUS, MARVELOUS, etc.) The flossy spelling OESOPHAGUS is also correct, but the simpler form is preferable and commoner—in OEDIPUS, on the other hand, the OE- spelling, reminiscent of its derivation from Greek mythology, prevails.

Write the word: ....

18. **ASSISTANT**
The double S comes first, then the single S.

Write the word: ....

19. **OBSESSION**
Because of words like POSSESSION and PREPOS-SESSING (see chapter 14), there is a great temptation to double the first S in OBSESSION. Resist the impulse—the word is formed from *session*, a sitting, plus the prefix *ob-*, on top; an OBSESSION etymologically sits on top of its victim, giving him no peace.

Write the word: ....

20. **PROFESSION**
We've already learned that PROFESSOR (chapter 13) has only one F, coming as it does from the verb to PROFESS. Ditto for PROFESSION.

Write the word: ....

21. **EMBARRASSMENT**
We've tackled this most plaguy of all spelling demons twice in the past (chapters 3 and 22), but it's worth looking at again. Note the double R (unlike HARASS and CARESS, each with a single R) *and* double S. And, of course, there's no E before the -MENT.

Write the word: ....

22. **HEMORRHAGE**

23. **CATARRH**

24. **DIARRHEA**
Note the unusual pattern of -RRH in these three medical terms. And note, too, the single T in CATARRH.

Write the words: ....

....

....

25. WOOLEN

26. WOLLY
These patterns seem contradictory and easily confused.
Both, of course, are derivatives of WOOL—for the
first, add the common ending -EN, hence one L; for
the second, add -LY, hence double L. (Technically
either word may be spelled with one L *or* two, and still
be correct—but the preferred, and recommended,
forms are WOOLEN and WOOLLY.)

Write the words: ....

....

27. EIGHTH
Yes, only one T, despite the fact that this is a combina-
tion of EIGHT and -TH. Like so many patterns in
English spelling, it's odd but it's true.

Write the word: ....

28. FEBRUARY
Some careless spellers omit the R because they ignore
it in pronunciation.

Write the word: ....

29. PLAYWRIGHT (a writer of plays)
WRIGHT is an old English suffix meaning worker or
creator; it is found also in *shipwright, wheelwright,
millwright,* etc. So, though a PLAYWRIGHT *writes*
plays, the word *write* does not appear in his title. (You
can, however, call a dramatist a *play-writer,* just as you
can call a novelist a *book-writer.*)

Write the word: ....

30. COPYRIGHT
A COPYRIGHT is an exclusive privilege or RIGHT.
And again, though written material is COPY-
RIGHTED, *write* does not appear in the word. (How-
ever, the man on a newspaper or in an advertising

agency who writes copy is a COPYWRITER.)

Write the word: ....

Let's Make the Correct Patterns Automatic

I. Fill in the missing letters, then rewrite the complete word.

1. WOO_EN	....	(L)
2. WOO__Y	....	(LL)
3. ESOPHAG_S	....	(U)
4. STIMUL_S	....	(U)
5. INCUB_S	....	(U)
6. OEDIP_S	....	(U)
7. IMPET_S	....	(U)
8. SARCOPHAG_S	....	(U)
9. MARVEL__S	....	(OU)
10. PRO_ESSION	....	(F)
11. PRO_ESSOR	....	(F)
12. OB_ESSION	....	(S)
13. PO__ESSION	....	(SS)
14. PREPO__ESSING	....	(SS)
15. A__ISTANT	....	(SS)
16. EMBA__A__MENT	....	(RR, SS)
17. FEB__ARY	....	(RU)
18. EIGH_H	....	(T)
19. COPY_IGHT	....	(R)
20. PLAY__IGHT	....	(WR)
21. HEMO__AGE	....	(RRH)

22. CATA____   .... (RRH)

23. DIA____EA   .... (RRH)

24. ASSI__TANT   .... (S)

25. EMBA____ASSING   .... (RR)

26. HA__ASS   .... (R)

27. CA__ESS   .... (R)

28. CA__ARRH   .... (T)

29. HIPPOPOTAM__S   .... (U)

30. __SOPHAGUS   .... (E)

31. __DIPUS   .... (OE)

32. A__IST   .... (SS)

33. OB__ESSIVE   .... (S)

II. Every word below is either misspelled or spelled in its less preferable form—cross it out and rewrite correctly in the recommended pattern.

1. opress

   ....   (OPPRESS)

2. plebian

   ....   (PLEBEIAN)

3. curvacious

   ....   (CURVACEOUS)

4. saphire

   ....   (SAPPHIRE)

5. wallnut

   ....   (WALNUT)

6. wellfare

....   (WELFARE)

7. wellcome

....   (WELCOME)

8. presumtuous

....   (PRESUMPTUOUS)

9. chagrinned

....   (CHAGRINED)

10. kidnapper

....   (KIDNAPER)

11. apochryphal

....   (APOCRYPHAL)

12. sychophant

....   (SYCOPHANT)

13. maccabre

....   (MACABRE)

14. crysanthemum

....   (CHRYSANTHEMUM)

15. marvellous

....   (MARVELOUS)

16. kidnapped

....   (KIDNAPED)

17. stimulous

....   (STIMULUS)

18. asistant

.... (ASSISTANT)

19. obssession

.... (OBSESSION)

20. proffession

.... (PROFESSION)

21. embarrased

.... (EMBARRASSED)

22. hemorrage

.... (HEMORRHAGE)

23. woollen

.... (WOOLEN)

24. eightth

.... (EIGHTH)

25. Febuary

.... (FEBRUARY)

26. playwrite

.... (PLAYWRIGHT)

27. copywright

.... (COPYRIGHT)

28. cattarrh

.... (CATARRH)

29. diarrea

.... (DIARRHEA)

30. esophagous

....   (ESOPHAGUS)

31. wooly

....   (WOOLLY)

32. marvelled

....   (MARVELED)

33. kidnapping

....   (KIDNAPING)

34. assisst

....   (ASSIST)

35. obssessive

....   (OBSESSIVE)

36. posession

....   (POSSESSION)

37. embarrassement

....   (EMBARRASSMENT)

38. proffessor

....   (PROFESSOR)

39. catarr

....   (CATARRH)

40. oesophagous

....   (ESOPHAGUS)

41. incubous

....   (INCUBUS)

42. oedipous

.... (OEDIPUS)

43. marvelling

.... (MARVELING)

44. opression

.... (OPPRESSION)

45. presumptious

.... (PRESUMPTUOUS)

46. chagrinning

.... (CHAGRINING)

47. sicophant

.... (SYCOPHANT)

48. macaber

.... (MACABRE)

49. harrass

.... (HARASS)

50. carress

.... (CARESS)

Chapter **40.**
MORE ON -ISE

At the very beginning of our work together, you learned that most verbs end in -IZE rather than -ISE, but that ten -ISE verbs were important. These ten, you will recall, were:

1. CHAST<u>ISE</u> ....
2. EXERC<u>ISE</u> ....
3. ADVERT<u>ISE</u> ....
4. ADV<u>ISE</u> ....
5. DESP<u>ISE</u> ....
6. DEV<u>ISE</u> ....
7. SUPERV<u>ISE</u> ....
8. IMPROV<u>ISE</u> ....
9. SURPR<u>ISE</u> ....
10. REV<u>ISE</u> ....

(Just as further, valuable practice, cover each one and rewrite it correctly.)

Then, in a later chapter, you discovered the two common -YZE verbs:

1. ANAL<u>YZE</u> ....
2. PARAL<u>YZE</u> ....

Today, we are interested in the remaining -ISE words that are likely to be misspelled. Work on the following:

1. ENTERPRISE ....

2. COMPRISE ....

3. APPRISE ....

4. SURMISE ....

5. COMPROMISE ....

6. DISGUISE ....

7. EXCISE ....

8. EXORCISE ....

9. INCISE ....

10. CIRCUMCISE ....

11. MERCHANDISE ....

12. FRANCHISE ....

If you can so tighten your visual memory, and with enough practice you will, that these twelve words, plus the ten studied earlier, look right *only* when ending in -ISE, never in -IZE, all possibility of confusion or error will vanish. For no other -ISE word is ever misspelled, even by the inexpert; and you will self-confidently spell all others (except, of course, ANALYZE and PARALYZE) with an -IZE ending.

So, let's get to work making the correct patterns of these 22 demons an integral, permanent, part of your brain-and-finger responses.

I. First, spend a few minutes carefully studying the two lists of -ISE words. When you feel quite familiar with them, see whether you can write at least 16 of them in the blanks below, relying only on memory and not checking back until you have finished. (If you can remember more than 16, your powers of recall are abnormal—write any additional examples in the margin of the page.)

1. ....   9. ....

2. ....   10. ....

3. ....   11. ....

4. ....   12. ....

5. ....   13. ....

6. ....   14. ....

7. ....   15. ....

8. ....   16. ....

II. Now fill in the missing letter or letters of these derived forms, then rewrite the complete words. Not all of them are -ISE examples, so look sharp!

1. REVIL_ED   .... (S)
2. REVI_ION   .... (S)
3. ADVI_ER   .... (S)
4. CHASTI_ED   .... (S)
5. CHASTI_EMENT   .... (S)
6. INCI_ED   .... (S)
7. INCI_ION   .... (S)
8. CIRCUMCI_ED   .... (S)
9. EXCI_ED   .... (S)
10. EXORCI_ED   .... (S)
11. EXCI_ION   .... (S)
12. SURMI_ING   .... (S)
13. ENTERPRI_ING   .... (S)
14. ANAL__E   .... (YZ)

15. MERCHANDI_ING .... (S)

16. DISGUI_ED .... (S)

17. REALI_ED .... (Z)

18. AUTHORI_ED .... (Z)

19. PARAL__E .... (YZ)

20. DEVI_ED .... (S)

21. SUPERVI_OR .... (S)

22. SURPRI_ING .... (S)

23. PATRONI_E .... (Z)

24. RECOGNI_ED .... (Z)

25. FRANCHI_ED .... (S)

26. ENFRANCHI_E .... (S)

27. DISENFRANCHI_E .... (S)

28. MINIMI_E .... (Z)

29. COMPROMI_ING .... (S)

30. SYMPATHI_ING .... (Z)

31. COMPRI_ED .... (S)

32. APPRI_ED .... (S)

33. ADVERTI_ER .... (S)

34. ADVERTI__MENT .... (SE)

35. DESPI_ED .... (S)

36. EXERCI_ES .... (S)

37. ANAL_SIS .... (Y)

38. PARAL_SIS .... (Y)

39. IMPROVI_ED .... (S)

40. EMPHASI_E .... (Z)

41. CAPSI_E .... (Z)

42. APOLOGI_E .... (Z)

43. ANAL_ST .... (Y)

44. PARAL_TIC .... (Y)

45. ADVI_ING .... (S)

46. SUPERVI_ION .... (S)

47. PSYCHOANAL__E .... (YZ)

48. COMPROMI_ED .... (S)

49. ENTERPRI_ES .... (S)

50. IMPROVI_ATION .... (S)

Chapter 41.

FIFTH REVIEW TEST

I. Fill in the missing letters, then rewrite each word.

1. INCEN_E .... (S)
2. ADOLE__ENT .... (SC)
3. UNCON__IOUS .... (SC)
4. DEFEN_E .... (S)
5. IRIDE__ENT .... (SC)
6. CON__IOUS .... (SC)
7. VI_IOUS .... (C)
8. VI__ERA .... (SC)
9. PRETEN_E .... (S)
10. AB__ESS .... (SC)
11. LA__IVIOUS .... (SC)
12. RESU__ITATE .... (SC)
13. CON__IENCE .... (SC)
14. OFFEN_E .... (S)
15. OMNI__IENCE .... (SC)
16. LL_EN_E .... (C, S)
17. SUSPEN_E .... (S)
18. CONVALE__ENT .... (SC)

19. LU__IOUS   .... (SC)

20. AB_ENCE   .... (S)

II. Each word below has been deliberately misspelled. Rewrite it correctly.

1. acceed

.... (ACCEDE)

2. succede

.... (SUCCEED)

3. supercede

.... (SUPERSEDE)

4. proceedure

.... (PROCEDURE)

5. preceed

.... (PRECEDE)

6. excede

.... (EXCEED)

7. putrify

.... (PUTREFY)

8. analize

.... (ANALYZE)

9. ecstacy

.... (ECSTASY)

10. hypocracy

.... (HYPOCRISY)

11. stupifying

.... (STUPEFYING)

12. trafficing

.... (TRAFFICKING)

13. brocolli

.... (BROCCOLI)

14. morroco

.... (MOROCCO)

15. liquifaction

.... (LIQUEFACTION)

16. mocassin

.... (MOCCASIN)

17. idiosyncricy

.... (IDIOSYNCRASY)

18. purefy

.... (PURIFY)

19. picollo

.... (PICCOLO)

20. picallili

.... (PICCALILLI)

21. bucaneer

.... (BUCCANEER)

22. mimicer

.... (MIMICKER)

23. apostacy

....   (APOSTASY)

24. rarify

....   (RAREFY)

25. paralize

....   (PARALYZE)

III. Find the one misspelled word in each trio, and rewrite it correctly.

1. mezzanine, quizes, Sabbath.

....   (QUIZZES)

2. acommodate, committee, cinnamon.

....   (ACCOMMODATE)

3. reconnaissance, corobborate, millennium.

....   (CORROBORATE)

4. harass, caress, embarass.

....   (EMBARRASS)

5. recconoiter, immaculate, macaroon.

....   (RECONNOITER)

6. hazard, mayonnaise, tocatta.

....   (TOCCATA)

7. raccoon, maccaroni, connoisseur.

....   (MACARONI)

8. pizzicatto, obbligato,
   accumulate.

   ....   (PIZZICATO)

9. accrue, accordian,
   accommodate.

   ....   (ACCORDION)

10. accoustics, across, accost.

    ....   (ACOUSTICS)

11. aggravate, aggree, aggrieved.

    ....   (AGREE)

12. agressive, disagree, aggregate.

    ....   (AGGRESSIVE)

13. allege, alotted, allure.

    ....   (ALLOTTED)

14. opressive, plebeian, sapphire.

    ....   (OPPRESSIVE)

15. walnut, presumptuous,
    curvacious.

    ....   (CURVACEOUS)

16. welcome, wellfare, marvelous.

    ....   (WELFARE)

17. chagrined, kidnaped,
    maccabre.

    ....   (MACABRE)

18. apochryphal, sycophant,
    chrysanthemum.

    ....   (APOCRYPHAL)

19. esophagus, stimulus,
    rhinocerus.

....   (RHINOCEROS)

20. assistant, obssession,
    possession.

....   (OBSESSION)

21. profession, embarrassement,
    harassment.

....   (EMBARRASSMENT)

22. hemorrhage, diarrhea,
    cattarrh.

....   (CATARRH)

23. woolen, woolly, Febuary.

....   (FEBRUARY)

24. copyright, playright,
    eighth.

....   (PLAYWRIGHT)

25. realize, advertize, authorize.

....   (ADVERTISE)

IV. Fill in the missing letter or letters, then rewrite the complete word.

1. CHASTI_E   ....   (S)

2. SURPRI_E   ....   (S)

3. REVI_E   ....   (S)

4. ANAL__E   ....   (YZ)

5. NEUTRALI_E   ....   (Z)

6. DISGUI_E   .... (S)

7. PARAL__E   .... (YZ)

8. LOCALI_E   .... (Z)

9. COMPROMI_E   .... (S)

10. SURMI_E   .... (S)

11. PLAGIARI_E   .... (Z)

12. COMPRI_E   .... (S)

13. ENTERPRI_E   .... (S)

14. APPRI_E   .... (S)

15. IMPROVI_E   .... (S)

16. CAPITALI_E   .... (Z)

17. EXERCI_E   .... (S)

18. DESPI_E   .... (S)

19. ITALICI_E   .... (Z)

20. SUPERVI_E   .... (S)

Chapter 42.

MORE HOMONYMS

Let us consider, today, some more homonyms that are subject to confusion and misspelling.

Homonyms, you will recall, are words with similar or identical pronunciations, but different meanings and spelling patterns—*gate* and *gait*, *aisle* and *isle*, *they're*, *their* and *there*, *whose* and *who's*, *its* and *it's*, etc.

1. ITS—IT'S
   ITS (no apostrophe) is possessive—the cat licked ITS paws; the baby played with ITS toes; etc.

   IT'S (note the apostrophe) means IT IS—IT'S raining today; IT'S an ill wind that blows no good; etc.

   Bear in mind that possessive personal pronouns are not decorated with an apostrophe (*his, ours, theirs,* etc.), though possessive nouns are (*George's, Kitty's, Paul's,* etc.).

2. WHOSE—WHO'S
   It would logically follow, then, that WHOSE (no apostrophe) is possessive—WHOSE little girl are you?; the man WHOSE wife he stole; etc.

   WHO'S (note the apostrophe) is a contraction of WHO IS—the man WHO'S *(who is)* coming to dinner; WHO'S *(who is)* absent today?; etc.

3. THEIR—THEY'RE—THERE
   THEIR is a possessive pronoun like ITS, HIS, HER, OUR—they took THEIR time, didn't they?, we found THEIR money, etc. An S is added (but no apostrophe) when the noun is omitted—they'll get THEIRS, they have THEIRS but we don't have ours yet, etc.

THEY'RE, like IT'S and WHO'S, is spelled with an apostrophe to denote the omission of a letter, in this case A—the word is a contraction of THEY ARE. THEY'RE happy now THEY'RE home, etc.

THERE shows direction—let's go THERE—or is used in patterns like: who's THERE?, THERE is no way to tell, THERE are no atheists in foxholes, etc.

When THERE IS or THERE ARE is written as a contraction, an apostrophe is required: THERE'S, THERE'RE: THERE'S no way to tell, THERE'RE no atheists in foxholes.

4. COMPLIMENT—COMPLEMENT
The first spelling, with the I, is for the word that means light praise—he COMPLIMENTED his wife on how well she managed on the little money he gave her.

COMPLEMENT—with an E—derives from the verb to COMPLETE. Anything which helps bring something to completion, or which, with something, forms a whole, is a COMPLEMENT to it. COMPLEMENT is also a verb—the adjective is COMPLEMENTARY.

5. CAPITAL—CAPITOL
A *city* which is the seat of government of a territory is the CAPITAL—Albany is the CAPITAL of New York, Washington is the CAPITAL of the U.S. CAPITOL designates the *building* in which a state legislature holds its sessions—with a capital C, the word refers to the building in which the U.S. Congress meets.

6. FIANCÉ—FIANCÉE
One E for the man, two EE's for the woman, to whom someone is engaged to be married. The two words are pronounced identically (fee-ahn-SAY), and the accent mark always falls on the first of the two E's, if there are two.

So, that's clear enough, isn't it? Let's try some sentences. Check the correct form of each word.

1. (a) It's, (b) Its a cold day in August when
   he lends anyone money.   (a)
2. Every period has (a) it's, (b) its favorite
   songs.   (b)
3. I know (a) whose, (b) who's making all
   that noise.   (b)
4. (a) Whose, (b) Who's your favorite film
   star?   (b)
5. (a) Whose, (b) Who's book are you using?   (a)
6. (a) Their, (b) They're, (c) There no
   friends of mine.   (b)
7. (a) Their, (b) There is no fool like an old
   fool.   (b)
8. We found (a) their, (b) there work unsat-
   isfactory.   (a)
9. Plagiarism is the highest form of
   (a) compliment, (b) complement.   (a)
10. This little hat really (a) compliments,
    (b) complements her outfit.   (b)
11. Springfield is the (a) capitol, (b) capital
    of Illinois.   (b)
12. The (a) capitol, (b) capital at Providence
    is topped with a beautiful dome.   (a)
13. Her (a) fiancé, (b) fiancée is ugly but rich.   (a)
14. His (a) fiancé, (b) fiancée is the most
    beautiful girl I've ever seen—but poor.   (b)

Consider six more sets of homonyms.

7. LOOSE—LOSE

Only approximate homonyms, LOOSE is pronounced
with a hissed S, and rhymes with *moose*, LOSE has a
buzzed S and rhymes with *choose*. But it is startling
how often spellers write one when they mean the other.

LOOSE is an adjective, the opposite of *tight*—his
arms hung LOOSE; or, occasionally, a verb meaning to
untie, set loose, etc.—"LOOSE my hands," he begged.
The more common form of this verb is LOOSEN.

LOSE is only a verb—to LOSE one's way, they
LOSE their chance, etc.

8. NAV<u>A</u>L—NAV<u>E</u>L

   NAV<u>A</u>L refers to a navy—NAV<u>A</u>L battles, etc.

   NAV<u>E</u>L is the spelling for the anatomical depression less elegantly known as a bellybutton, or for any similarly shaped indentation, as in a NAV<u>E</u>L orange.

9. TWO—TOO—TO

   TWO is the number.
   TOO is an adverb meaning either *also* or *excessively*.
   TO is a preposition.

   The following sentences illustrate the different uses of the three words:

   a. TWO men TO each woman are one TOO many; women, TOO, agree with this sentiment.
   b. He, TOO, knows TWO ways TO go home.
   c. He was TOO tired TO listen TO the TWO lectures.

10. YOUR—YOU'RE

    As in the case of ITS—IT'S, WHOSE—WHO'S, etc., the word without the apostrophe (YOUR) is a possessive pronoun, the one with the apostrophe (YOU'RE) is a contraction of pronoun and verb. The words are used thus: YOU'RE *(you are)* late; take off YOUR hat.

11. YO<u>LK</u>—YO<u>KE</u>

    YO<u>LK</u> is the yellow of an egg; YO<u>KE</u> is the spelling for any other meaning.

12. DYE—DIE

    To DYE something is to change its color—the past tense is spelled DYED, the participle is DYEING.

    To DIE, or lose one's life, is DIED in the past, DYING in the participle.

Can you check the correct word in each sentence?

1. How did you (a) loose, (b) lose your
   money?   (b)
2. This knot is too (a) loose, (b) lose.   (a)
3. Lord Nelson was a famous (a) naval,
   (b) navel officer.   (a)

4. Have you been (a) two, (b) too, (c) to
   the store?   (c)
5. He's (a) two, (b) too, (c) to sick to leave
   the house.   (b)
6. Don't think (a) your (b) you're going to
   get away with that chicanery.   (b)
7. Few men will tolerate the (a) yoke (b) yolk
   of slavery.   (a)
8. If this dress were (a) died, (b) dyed blue,
   it would look prettier.   (b)
9. He's in the cleaning and (a) dyeing,
   (b) dying business.   (a)

Chapter 43.

TACKLING THE -ER, -OR PROBLEM

Most of us rely, and quite successfully, on our visual memory to decide whether to end a word with -ER or -OR.

Some very few words make us pause for a moment and think—and that's when we're lost, because if we don't reflexively and self-confidently tack the proper suffix to a root, -ER and -OR suddenly seem equally good.

Generally, if the root is, or comes from, a verb, the ending is -ER: *viewer, taker, user, worker, player, knitter, runner,* etc.

But this is not always so, as words like *depositor, conqueror, inheritor* and a number of other exceptions make only too clear.

What to do? Our best bet is to so familiarize ourselves with some of the commonly misspelled -OR forms, to get our minds so accustomed to thinking, and our fingers so accustomed to writing, -OR in these words, that we'll never be tempted to make that fatal pause.

For the most part, -ER words cause no difficulties.

So down to serious work on these -OR demons.

Examine each word, picture it, stare at it, let it set in your mind, then cover it and rewrite it.

1. SPECTAT**OR**   ....

2. INVEST**OR**   ....

3. INVENT**OR**   ....

4. ANCEST**OR**   ....

5. IMPOST**OR**   ....

6. DEPOSIT**OR** ....

7. EDUCAT**OR** ....

8. ELEVAT**OR** ....

9. ACCELERAT**OR** ....

10. INHERIT**OR** ....

11. SUPERVIS**OR** ....

12. SPECULAT**OR** ....

13. ESCALAT**OR** ....

14. SURVIV**OR** ....

15. CONQUER**OR** ....

16. INDICAT**OR** ....

17. CONSPIRAT**OR** ....

18. DISTRIBUT**OR** ....

19. CONTRIBUT**OR** ....

20. COMMENTAT**OR** ....

21. PROTECT**OR** ....

22. INVESTIGAT**OR** ....

23. PREDECESS**OR** ....

24. PREVARICAT**OR** ....

25. VISIT**OR** ....

26. ADMINISTRAT**OR** ....

27. ORAT**OR** ....

28. BACHEL**OR** ....

29. AVIAT**OR** ....

30. FABRICAT**OR** ....

Let's go around again, to make your responses even surer. Write the word that fits each definition.

1. He invents

   (I-) .... (INVENTOR)

2. He invests

   (I-) .... (INVESTOR)

3. He survives

   (S-) .... (SURVIVOR)

4. He educates

   (E-) .... (EDUCATOR)

5. He watches

   (S-) .... (SPECTATOR)

6. He conspires

   (C-) .... (CONSPIRATOR)

7. He investigates

   (I-) .... (INVESTIGATOR)

8. He pretends to be someone
   or something he isn't

   (I-) .... (IMPOSTOR)

9. He conquers

   (C-) .... (CONQUEROR)

10. It indicates

    (I-) .... (INDICATOR)

11. He speculates

    (S-) .... (SPECULATOR)

12. He distributes

(D-) .... (DISTRIBUTOR)

13. He deposits

(D-) .... (DEPOSITOR)

14. He inherits

(I-) .... (INHERITOR)

15. It elevates

(E-) .... (ELEVATOR)

16. He supervises

(S-) .... (SUPERVISOR)

17. Moving staircase

(E-) .... (ESCALATOR)

18. Forefather

(A-) .... (ANCESTOR)

19. It accelerates

(A-) .... (ACCELERATOR)

20. Liar

(F-) .... (FABRICATOR)

21. He protects

(P-) .... (PROTECTOR)

22. He contributes

(C-) .... (CONTRIBUTOR)

23. He comments on the news

(C-) .... (COMMENTATOR)

24. He flies

(A-) .... (AVIATOR)

25. He speaks in public

(O-) .... (ORATOR)

26. He is unmarried
(B-) .... (BACHELOR)

27. He comes before

(P-) .... (PREDECESSOR)

28. He tells fibs

(P-) .... (PREVARICATOR)

29. He pays a visit

(V-) .... (VISITOR)

30. He administers

(A-) .... (ADMINISTRATOR)

And now a third time to fix the -OR spellings permanently in your memory, to make them part of your reflexive finger reactions when you write. Add the proper ending to each root, then rewrite the complete word.

1. CONSPIRAT__   .... (OR)

2. INVENT__   .... (OR)

3. ADMINISTRAT__   .... (OR)

4. SPECTAT__   .... (OR)

5. ADVERTIS__   .... (ER)

6. DISTRIBUT__   .... (OR)

7. QUESTION__   .... (ER)

8. IMPOST__   .... (OR)

9. BEGINN___ .... (ER)

10. PREVARICAT___ .... (OR)

11. INVEST___ .... (OR)

12. THINK___ .... (ER)

13. DEPOSIT___ .... (OR)

14. VISIT___ .... (OR)

15. CONTRIBUT___ .... (OR)

16. MARCH___ .... (ER)

17. ANCEST___ .... (OR)

18. NEWCOM___ .... (ER)

19. EDUCAT___ .... (OR)

20. INVESTIGAT___ .... (OR)

21. CONQUER___ .... (OR)

22. INHERIT___ .... (OR)

23. PROTECT___ .... (OR)

24. GOSSIP___ .... (ER)

25. SURVIV___ .... (OR)

26. SELL___ .... (ER)

27. COMMENTAT___ .... (OR)

28. PREDECESS___ .... (OR)

29. PRISON___ .... (ER)

30. ACCELERAT___ .... (OR)

31. LEARN___ .... (ER)

32. SPECULAT___ .... (OR)

33. INDICAT___ .... (OR)

34. ORAT__ .... (OR)

35. ESCALAT__ .... (OR)

36. WRIT__ .... (ER)

37. SUPERVIS__ .... (OR)

38. BUTCH__ .... (ER)

39. ELEVAT__ .... (OR)

40. FABRICAT__ .... (OR)

41. ENGRAV__ .... (ER)

42. AVIAT__ .... (OR)

43. JEWEL__ .... (ER)

44. BACHEL__ .... (OR)

Sidelights

One who advises is preferably spelled ADVIS<u>ER</u>, though the -OR form is also acceptable.

One who bets is preferably a BETT<u>OR</u>, though the spelling *better* is technically correct.

One who begs is, of course, a BEG<u>GAR</u>—one of the very few words in this category ending in -AR.

Chapter 44.

ANOTHER 30 SUPER-DEMONS

If you are in the habit of spelling a word correctly, its common misspelling may look absolutely outrageous to you. As you cruise through today's list you may more times than not think to yourself, "Why, of course! How else can one spell it!" But each word is a demon, each contains a trap for the unwary, each has a pitfall that the poor or mediocre speller stumbles over; so every now and again, the frequency depending on how good you are, you may be moved to exclaim, "I would never think it's spelled *that* way!"

Look sharp, be conscientious, train your mind and fingers carefully on any of the following you're not perfectly sure of. And rewrite even the words you're certain you'd never misspell.

1. GRAMMAR
   Poor GRAM<u>MAR</u> can MAR your speech—avoid -ER in the last syllable.

   Write the word: ....

2. CALENDAR
   There *is* a word *calender*, meaning a special kind of machine or a wandering dervish—but the chart that tells us the date ends in -AR.

   Write the word: ....

3. BEGGAR
   Another -AR word, as you will recall from the previous chapter.

   Write the word: ....

4. SERGEANT
   Two places to go wrong, and many people slip up on both. We *say* SAR-jent, but don't spell it that way.

   Write the word: ....

5. LIEUTENANT
   That French -LIEU combination is a bit slippery, especially since we pronounce it *loo-*.

   Write the word: ....

6. ADDRESS
   Watch that double D.

   Write the word: ....

7. APARTMENT
   Some spellers have a fondness for a double P here—but the word is simply APART plus -MENT.

   Write the word: ....

8. AWKWARD
   With a W following the K, it's easy to forget the one preceding it.

   Write the word: ....

9. BENEFIT
   You'd be amazed how many spellers think that underlined letter is an I. (You, too?) It isn't. Similar, therefore, is BENEFICIAL. And with the accent on the first syllable, the T- is, of course, never doubled: BENE-FITING, BENEFITED.

   Write the word: ....

10. CHALLENGE
This one may puzzle you, but school and college compositions have the word misspelled as *challange*.

Write the word: ....

11. ESCAPE
Of course the second letter is not an X—but some people think it is!

Write the word: ....

12. TUESDAY
-UE, not the other way around.

Write the word: ....

13. MERINGUE
M is the only letter most spellers are sure of in this word, which is mispronounced in so many different ways (including lemon MORAN pie) that it's no wonder misspellings are equally common. Say me-RANG.

Write the word: ....

14. COLE SLAW
Let's stay with food for a moment. This is a slaw made of COLE, a family of plants that includes cabbage. True, it's *served* COLD, but not spelled that way.

Write the word: ....

15. SAUERKRAUT
We use the German spelling of *sour* in this German dish.

Write the word: ....

16. SAUERBRATEN
And again in this one.

Write the word: ....

17. REVEILLE
Pronounced REV-e-lee, this French word is nevertheless spelled as indicated.

Write the word: ....

18. PHILIPPINES
The P, *not* the L, is doubled. But a native of the Islands is a FILIPINO—*one* L, *one* P.

Write the word: ....

19. DOESN'T
DOES plus NOT, an apostrophe replacing the missing O; many youngsters in elementary school, suiting the letters to the sound, write it *dosent*.

Write the word: ....

20. SOPHOMORE
We rarely say the underlined O—we must always write it.

Write the word: ....

21. HORS D'OEUVRES
The common American pronunciation of this plural French term would never indicate the correct pattern of letters, so take a permanent photograph of the OEUV- to store in your visual memory.

Write the word: ....

22. MANEUVER
This word is built on the same French stem as HORS D'OEUVRES, but you will be happy to hear that the spelling has been Anglicized, and the old-fashioned *manoeuvre* is no longer really current.

Write the word: ....

23. ATHLETIC
No A following the TH-, though a common mispro-

nunciation of the word often leads to such a misspelling. Likewise A<u>TH</u>LETE.

Write the word: ....

24. DILE<u>MM</u>A
Note the double M; no N in the word.

Write the word: ....

25. COMPLE<u>X</u>ION
One of the very few words in American spelling ending in -XION. Most others (*inflection, connection, rejection,* etc.) have the -CTION pattern.

Write the word: ....

26. CHARA<u>C</u>TERISTIC
There are some who get carried away and put a second, unnecessary H after the second C, having properly used one after the first C. Likewise CHARA<u>CT</u>ER.

Write the word: ....

27. CELE<u>B</u>RATE
One L only.

Write the word: ....

28. CON<u>S</u>EN<u>S</u>US
All S's in this word after the first C.

Write the word: ....

29. S<u>Y</u>NON<u>Y</u>MOUS
-NYM is a common Greek prefix found in SYNO-N<u>Y</u>M, ANTON<u>Y</u>M, HOMON<u>Y</u>M, PSEUDON<u>Y</u>M, etc. The adjective forms retain the Y: SYNON<u>Y</u>-MOUS, ANTON<u>Y</u>MOUS, HOMON<u>Y</u>MOUS, PSEU-DON<u>Y</u>MOUS, etc. And note the first Y, also, in S<u>Y</u>NON<u>Y</u>MOUS.

Write the word: ....

30. UNANIMOUS

But in this word, built on a totally different, and Latin, root, an ending with a similar sound is spelled with an I.

Write the word: ....

Do you have these 30 words under tight control? If so, you'll have no difficulty filling in the missing letter or letters, then rewriting the complete word.

1. GRAMM_R   .... (A)

2. CALEND_R   .... (A)

3. BEGG_R   .... (A)

4. S_RGEANT   .... (E)

5. L___TENANT   .... (IEU)

6. A___RESS   .... (DD)

7. A_ARTMENT   .... (P)

8. A__WARD   .... (WK)

9. BEN_FIT   .... (E)

10. BEN_FICIAL   .... (E)

11. CHALL_NGE   .... (E)

12. E_CAPE   .... (S)

13. T__SDAY   .... (UE)

14. M_RINGUE   .... (E)

15. COL_ SLAW   .... (E)

16. S___RKRAUT   .... (AUE)

17. S___RBRATEN   .... (AUE)

18. REV__LLE   .... (EI)

19. PHILI__INES   .... (PP)
20. FILL__INO   .... (P)
21. DO__SN'T   .... (E)
22. SOPH__MORE   .... (O)
23. HORS D'___VRES   .... (OEU)
24. MAN__VER   .... (EU)
25. ATH__ETE   .... (L)
26. DILE__A   .... (MM)
27. COMPLE__ION   .... (X)
28. CHARA__TERISTIC .... (C)
29. CE__EBRATE   .... (L)
30. CON__ENSUS   .... (S)
31. SYNON__MOUS   .... (Y)
32. UNAN__MOUS   .... (I)
33. SERG__NT   .... (EA)
34. BENEFI__ED   .... (T)
35. MER__NGUE   .... (I)
36. PHI__IPPINES   .... (L)
37. FI__IPINO   .... (L)
38. HORS D'OEU___S   .... (VRE)
39. MANEUV__   .... (ER)
40. ATH__ETIC   .... (L)
41. CE__EBRATION   .... (L)
42. CHARA__TER   .... (C)
43. S__NONYMOUS   .... (Y)

44. UN—IMOUS .... (AN)

All right? Let's try it once more, with feeling. I'll deliberately misspell each word—you cross it out and write it correctly.

1. grammer

.... (GRAMMAR)

2. calender

.... (CALENDAR)

3. begger

.... (BEGGAR)

4. sargent

.... (SERGEANT)

5. lootenant

.... (LIEUTENANT)

6. adress

.... (ADDRESS)

7. appartment

.... (APARTMENT)

8. akward

.... (AWKWARD)

9. benifit

.... (BENEFIT)

10. benificial

.... (BENEFICIAL)

11. challange

....   (CHALLENGE)

12. excape

....   (ESCAPE)

13. Teusday

....   (TUESDAY)

14. marangue

....   (MERINGUE)

15. cold slaw

....   (COLE SLAW)

16. sourkraut

....   (SAUERKRAUT)

17. sourbraten

....   (SAUERBRATEN)

18. revellee

....   (REVEILLE)

19. Phillipines

....   (PHILIPPINES)

20. Fillipino

....   (FILIPINO)

21. dosent

....   (DOESN'T)

22. sophmore

....   (SOPHOMORE)

23. hors d'oevres

.... (HORS D'OEUVRES)

24. manuever

.... (MANEUVER)

25. athalete

.... (ATHLETE)

26. athaletic

.... (ATHLETIC)

27. dilemna

.... (DILEMMA)

28. complection

.... (COMPLEXION)

29. charachteristic

.... (CHARACTERISTIC)

30. cellebrate

.... (CELEBRATE)

31. concensus

.... (CONSENSUS)

32. synonimous

.:................................... (SYNONYMOUS)

33. unanamous

.... (UNANIMOUS)

Chapter 45.

FUN WITH FINAL Y

As everyone knows, Y at the end of a word often changes to I when letters are added.

Thus, CRY becomes CRIES, CRIER, and CRIED; LIVELY becomes LIVELIER and LIVELIEST; STEADY becomes STEADILY; LAZY becomes LAZILY, LAZINESS, LAZIER, and LAZIEST; BEAUTY becomes BEAUTIFUL; WORRY becomes WORRIMENT; WEARY becomes WEARIES, WEARIED, WEARINESS, and WEARILY; FLY becomes FLIES; SKY becomes SKIES; DIARY becomes DIARIES; LADY becomes LADIES; and so on, indefinitely.

This change occurs so frequently and is so accepted and unconfusing a part of English spelling, that it is only *when terminal Y remains unchanged* that any problem creeps in.

And it is the *lack of change* we shall briefly explore today.

I. When terminal Y is preceded by a *vowel (monkey, boy, day, relay*, etc.), S or -ED is added directly, *Y remaining unchanged.*

Practice on these, noting the vowel preceding the Y in each instance.

WRITE THE
SECOND WORD HERE

1. VALLEY—VALLEYS   ....

2. MONKEY—MONKEYS   ....

3. DONKEY—DONKEYS   ....

 4. KEY—KEYS   ....

 5. BOY—BOYS   ....

 6. ATTORNEY—ATTORNEYS ....

 7. RELAY—RELAYS   ....

 8. MONEY—MONEYS   ....
    (However, though violating the principle, the plural of
    MONEY is often written MONIES; but the less com-
    mon MONEYS is theoretically preferable.)

 9. BETRAY—BETRAYED   ....

10. DESTROY—DESTROYS   ....

11. ENJOY—ENJOYMENT   ....

12. PLAY—PLAYED   ....

13. COY—COYLY   ....

14. GRAY—GRAYER   ....

15. PRAY—PRAYER   ....

II. Needless to say, there are a few exceptions, most of
which you're likely to spell correctly without thinking of
rules. Just to be sure, practice the following.

16. GAY—GAILY   ....
    (Preferable to *gayly*, which is also correct, but not
    recommended.)

17. GAY—GAIETY   ....
    (Preferable to *gayety*, though the latter is also accept-
    able.)

18. LAY—LAID   ....

19. SAY—SAID   ....

20. PAY—PAID   ....

III. If a word has only one syllable, final Y is unchanged before -NESS and -LY. Before other suffixes, Y does change to I.

21. DRY—DRYNESS   ....

22. DRY—DRYLY   ....

23. COY—COYNESS   ....

24. SHY—SHYNESS   ....

25. SHY—SHYLY   ....

26. SLY—SLYNESS   ....

27. SLY—SLYLY   ....

28. SPRY—SPRYNESS   ....

29. SPRY—SPRYLY   ....

30. WRY—WRYNESS   ....

31. WRY—WRYLY   ....

32. DRY—DRIER   ....

33. DRY—DRIES   ....

34. TRY—TRIED   ....

35. FLY—FLIER   ....

(*Drily, shily, slily* are theoretically also correct, but not recommended; FLYER is an acceptable variant of FLIER; and though DRIER is the only permissible spelling for the adjective—the climate is DRIER than we expected—either DRIER or DRYER may be used as a noun, for example, a machine that dries clothes.)

IV. If a proper name ends in Y, the plural merely adds S.

36. HARRY—HARRYS   ....

37. MARY—MARYS   ....

38. McCARTHY—McCARTHYS ....

V. Before -ING, Y is, of course, unchanged, since to change it would result in two successive I's.

39. WORRY—WORRYING   ....
40. FLY—FLYING   ....
41. DRY—DRYING   ....
42. BUSY—BUSYING   ....
43. BEAUTIFY—BEAUTIFYING ....
44. STUPEFY—STUPEFYING   ....

Are the important rules clear to you? Try these exercises.

I. Complete each statement.

1. Final Y generally changes to ....   (I)
   before the addition of a suffix.

2. But (as in *boy, day, valley,* etc.) if
   final Y is preceded by a ....,   (vowel)
   it is unchanged.

3. In one-syllable words, final Y remains
   unchanged before -NESS and .....   (-LY)

4. In one-syllable words, final Y remains
   unchanged before -LY and ....   (-NESS)

5. Final Y of a proper name remains
   .... when S is added.   (unchanged)

6. Final Y never changes before ....   (-ING)

7. The past of LAY is ....   (LAID)

8. The past of SAY is.........   (SAID)

9. The past of PAY is ....   (PAID)

10. The past of PLAY is............   (PLAYED)

11. Adding -NESS to DRY results in

....   (DRYNESS)

12. Adding -LY to DRY results in ....   (DRYLY)

13. Adding -LY to GAY results in ....   (GAILY)

14. Adding -ETY to GAY results in ....   (GAIETY)

II. Write the word that results when the indicated letter or letters are added.

1. FLY plus -S

....   (FLIES)

2. HAPPY plus -LY

....   (HAPPILY)

3. BUSY plus -ER

....   (BUSIER)

4. LONELY plus -EST

....   (LONELIEST)

5. BEAUTY plus -FY

....   (BEAUTIFY)

6. WORRY plus -MENT

....   (WORRIMENT)

7. WEARY plus -NESS

....   (WEARINESS)

8. SKY plus -S

.... (SKIES)

9. SILLY plus -NESS

.... (SILLINESS)

10. BODY plus -S

.... (BODIES)

11. STORY plus -S

.... (STORIES)

12. DUTY plus -S

.... (DUTIES)

13. LIVELY plus -ER

.... (LIVELIER)

14. VALLEY plus -S

.... (VALLEYS)

15. DONKEY plus -S

.... (DONKEYS)

16. COY plus -LY

.... (COYLY)

17. ATTORNEY plus -S

.... (ATTORNEYS)

18. MONEY plus -ED

.... (MONEYED)

19. MONKEY plus -ED

.... (MONKEYED)

20. GAY plus -LY

....   (GAILY)

21. GAY plus -ETY

....   (GAIETY)

22. SHY plus -LY

....   (SHYLY)

23. DRY plus -LY

....   (DRYLY)

24. DRY plus -NESS

....   (DRYNESS)

25. DRY plus -ER (adj.)

....   (DRIER)

26. DRY plus -EST

....   (DRIEST)

27. WRY plus -ER

....   (WRIER)

28. WRY plus -LY

....   (WRYLY)

29. WRY plus -EST

....   (WRIEST)

30. MURPHY plus -S

....   (MURPHYS)

31. SAMMY plus -S

....   (SAMMYS)

32. MONKEY plus -ING

.... (MONKEYING)

33. BEAUTIFY plus -ING

.... (BEAUTIFYING)

34. ACCOMPANY plus -ED

.... (ACCOMPANIED)

35. ACCOMPANY plus -ING

.... (ACCOMPANYING)

36. ACCOMPANY plus -ES

.... (ACCOMPANIES)

37. DRY plus -ING

.... (DRYING)

38. KEY plus -S

.... (KEYS)

39. MERRY plus -EST

.... (MERRIEST)

40. MERRY plus -LY

.... (MERRILY)

41. FAIRY plus -S

.... (FAIRIES)

42. COMPANY plus -S

.... (COMPANIES)

43. LAY plus -D

.... (LAID)

44. SAY plus -D

....   (SAID)

45. PAY plus -D

....   (PAID)

46. PLAY plus -D

....   (PLAYED)

47. PAY plus -ER

....   (PAYER)

48. PLAY plus -ER

....   (PLAYER)

49. SOOTHSAY plus -ER

....   (SOOTHSAYER)

50. FLY plus -ER

....   (FLIER)

51. BEAUTIFY plus -ER

....   (BEAUTIFIER)

52. GRAY plus -EST

....   (GRAYEST)

53. PRAY plus -ING

....   (PRAYING)

54. PRAY plus -ER

....   (PRAYER)

55. PRETTY plus -ER

....   (PRETTIER)

56. PRETTY plus -EST

....   (PRETTIEST)

57. PRETTY plus -NESS

....   (PRETTINESS)

58. PRETTY plus -LY

....   (PRETTILY)

59. GRAY plus -NESS

....   (GRAYNESS)

60. WOOLLY plus -NESS

....   (WOOLLINESS)

61. MARRY plus -ED

....   (MARRIED)

62. APPLY plus -ED

....   (APPLIED)

63. HURRY plus -S

....   (HURRIES)

64. TINY plus -ER

....   (TINIER)

65. PARTY plus -S

....   (PARTIES)

Chapter 46.

A FEW MINOR, BUT PESKY, SPELLING PROBLEMS

As we draw toward the close of our work together, let's cover some of the minor categories that we have not yet looked at.

I. A recurrent problem is whether to pluralize a noun ending in O *(banjo, hero, tomato)* by adding S, or -ES. The simplest, and also the most efficient, way to tackle this category is to concentrate on the 14 common words that *must* be pluralized by the addition of -ES only, and in all other cases merely tack on an S. The following plural forms, in which only the -ES spelling is permissible, should become as familiar to you as your own name and address. Study each one carefully, commit it to memory, then cover and rewrite.

1. (tomato) TOMATOES ....

2. (hero) HEROES ....

3. (potato) POTATOES ....

4. (echo) ECHOES ....

5. (mosquito) MOSQUITOES ....

6. (motto) MOTTOES ....

7. (veto) VETOES ....

8. (no) NOES ....

9. (torpedo) TORPEDOES ....

10. (Negro) NEGROES   ....

11. (embargo) EMBARGOES   ....

12. (innuendo) INNUENDOES   ....

13. (mulatto) MULATTOES   ....

14. (manifesto) MANIFESTOES   ....

Some others *may* be pluralized in -OES, but are correct also in -OS; many more are pluralized only in -OS. So get on intimate terms with the 14 listed, and blithely pluralize every other by simply adding S.

Can you, before we continue, think of at least eight of these -OES plurals? Write them below, in any order, without looking at the preceding list, then check your results.

1. ....   5. ....

2. ....   6. ....

3. ....   7. ....

4. ....   8. ....

II. As you will recall, the consonant G is pronounced "soft" (i.e., like a J) before E, as in *gem, outrage, charge*, etc., but "hard" (as in *go*) before an O. Hence, in all the following, since the G is "soft," the vowel E must precede the suffix -OUS.

15. GORGEOUS   ....

16. COURAGEOUS   ....

17. OUTRAGEOUS   ....

18. UMBRAGEOUS   ....

19. ADVANTAGEOUS   ....

20. DISADVANTAGEOUS   ....

21. RAMPAGEOUS   ....

In the following, the vowel I is used to "soften" the G before -OUS.

22. CONTAGIOUS ....

23. RELIGIOUS ....

24. IRRELIGIOUS ....

25. SACRILEGIOUS ....

26. EGREGIOUS ....
(pronounced e-GREE-jus)

In the noun forms of the first three of the foregoing, the I serves to "soften" the G before -ON.

27. CONTAGION ....

28. RELIGION ....

29. IRRELIGION ....

And in the following, E "softens" the G before -ON:

30. PIGEON ....

31. BLUDGEON ....

32. DUNGEON ....

Some of these words we have already worked on in an earlier chapter—RELIGIOUS, SACRILEGIOUS, PIGEON, etc.—but they are worth considering again.

Note, also, that the -GEOUS ending (examples 16-21) attaches to words the last syllable of which is -AGE: *courage, outrage, umbrage, advantage, disadvantage, rampage.*

III. Like so many endings, -ARY, -ERY also presents problems. For the most part, there is a greater temptation to use -ERY when -ARY is correct than the other way around. (There's certainly no doubt in words like CUTLERY, NUNNERY, FINERY, BREWERY, BAKERY, BRIB-

ERY, FLATTERY, THIEVERY, etc.) This problem, too, we shall attack in a simple and efficient manner—we'll learn the few possibly confusing -ERY forms and feel self-assured in ending every other doubtful word with -ARY.

So get on good terms with these -ERY words—study, cover, then rewrite each one.

33. MONASTERY   ....

34. CEMETERY   ....

35. MILLINERY   ....

36. CONFECTIONERY   ....

37. DYSENTERY   ....

38. LAMASERY   ....

(We already know that STATIONERY may also be spelled STATIONARY, depending on the meaning.)

DYSENTERY, by the way, is a kind of intestinal disease —note, also, the unusual DYS- prefix; LAMASERY is a Buddhist monastery.

Have you made lasting friends with these six -ERY forms? Study them once more, then, without reference to the list, see whether you can write all six, in any order, below.

1. ....   4. ....

2. ....   5. ....

3. ....   6. ....

Keep in mind, then, that if a word is not one of our six -ERY specials, and you have any doubt as to its spelling, the probability is overwhelming that -ARY is the correct ending. For example:

39. DICTIONARY   ....

40. SECRETARY   ....

41. SECOND<u>ARY</u>   ....

42. ADVERS<u>ARY</u>   ....

43. ELEMENT<u>ARY</u>   ....

44. COMMENT<u>ARY</u>   ....

Ready to test the efficiency of your learning? Try the following exercises.

I. Pluralize each word, then rewrite it.

1. MOTTO   .... (OES)

2. ECHO   .... (OES)

3. INNUENDO   .... (OES)

4. AUTO   .... (OS)

5. NEGRO   .... (OES)

6. TOMATO   .... (OES)

7. EMBARGO   .... (OES)

8. MULATTO   .... (OES)

9. CELLO   .... (OS)

10. VETO   .... (OES)

11. PIANO   .... (OS)

12. HERO   .... (OES)

13. MOSQUITO   .... (OES)

14. EMBRYO   .... (OS)

15. POTATO   .... (OES)

16. RADIO   .... (OS)

17. ESKIMO   .... (OS)

18. BANJO   .... (OS)

19. STUDIO .... (OS)

20. NO .... (OES)

21. SOLO .... (OS)

22. MANIFESTO .... (OES)

23. HOBO .... (OS)

24. ZERO .... (OS)

25. TORPEDO .... (OES)

II. Complete the following words by supplying the missing letters, then rewrite.

1. GORG__US .... (EO)

2. COURAG__US .... (EO)

3. OUTRAG__US .... (EO)

4. UMBRAG__US .... (EO)

5. ADVANTAG__US .... (EO)

6. DISADVANTAG__US .... (EO)

7. RAMPAG__US .... (EO)

8. CONTAG__US .... (IO)

9. RELIG__US .... (IO)

10. IRRELIG__US .... (IO)

11. SACRILEG__US .... (IO)

12. EGREG__US .... (IO)

13. CONTAG__N .... (IO)

14. RELIG__N .... (IO)

15. IRRELIG__N .... (IO)

16. PIG__N .... (EO)

17. BLUDG__N .... (EO)

18. DUNG__N   .... (EO)

19. RELI__OUS   .... (GI)

20. IRRELI__OUS   .... (GI)

21. SACR_L_GIOUS   .... (I, E)

22. SACR_L_GE   .... (I, E)

23. PI_EON   .... (G)

24. BLU__EON   .... (DG)

25. DU__EON   .... (NG)

III. Add either -ARY or -ERY to each of the following roots, then rewrite the complete word.

1. SECRET-   .... (-ARY)

2. MONAST-   .... (-ERY)

3. DICTION-   .... (-ARY)

4. CEMET-   .... (-ERY)

5. CULIN-   .... (-ARY)

6. COMMENT-   .... (-ARY)

7. MILLIN-   .... (-ERY)

8. ELEMENT-   .... (-ARY)

9. CONFECTION-   .... (-ERY)

10. SECOND-   .... (-ARY)

11. TEMPOR-   .... (-ARY)

12. CUSTOM-   .... (-ARY)

13. SANCTU-   .... (-ARY)

14. LAMAS-   .... (-ERY)

15. DYSENT-   .... (-ERY)

Chapter 47.

TWENTY-ONE ADDITIONAL DEMONS

Today, we consider a number of words, some related, others quite unrelated, that plague the average speller. Study each one, note the underlined area or areas, read the explanatory note, then cover and rewrite.

1. MASSACRE
   Like ACRE, OGRE, and MACABRE, one of the very few words in American spelling ending in -RE. (Words like *saber, meager, maneuver,* etc., are, in England, commonly spelled *sabre, meagre, maneuvre,* etc.)

   Write the word: ....

2. GLAMOUR
   Although the adjective is GLAMOROUS, the noun has this uncommon ending. (British, not American, spelling is attached to -OUR—*humour, favour, honour,* etc. Stay away from it except in GLAMOUR.)

   Write the word: ....

3. GLAMOROUS
   See preceding note.

   Write the word: ....

4. LANGUOR
   Like LIQUOR, this word ends in the rare pattern -UOR.

   Write the word: ....

5. LINGERIE
Though many people pronounce the last syllable -RAY, the only spelling is as indicated.

Write the word: ....

6. WEDNESDAY
We say WENZ-dee, but spell it as shown.

Write the word: ....

7. NINTH
No E in this word, despite *nine, nineteen,* and *ninety*.

Write the word: ....

8. WINTRY
This spelling is preferable to *wintery*.

Write the word: ....

9. ILLITERATE
An UNLETTERED person is ILLITERATE—note that E follows a T in both words. The noun is ILLITERACY.

Write the word: ....

10. LEGITIMATE
Note the two underlined I's. The negative is ILLEGITIMATE.

Write the word: ....

11. TEMPERAMENT
Note the underlined A, often omitted in pronunciation.

Write the word: ....

12. LICORICE
Not *licorish,* though some people, retaining childhood patterns of pronunciation, say it that way.

Write the word: ....

13. COURTESY
COURTESY is the good manners originally practiced
at COURT. Note the E, also, as in COURTEOUS.

Write the word: ....

14. RHAPSODY
The H is silent, but must appear in writing.

Write the word: ....

15. INSTALL
Note the double L, which should be kept in the noun
INSTALLMENT, though *instalment* is technically also
correct.

Write the word: ....

16. APPALL
Note the double P.

Write the word: ....

17. ENTHRALL
This spelling is far preferable to *enthral*, as is also the
similar pattern in the noun ENTHRALLMENT.

Write the word: ....

18. FULFILL

19. INSTILL

20. DISTILL
These three words may technically be written ending in
one L, but avoid such a pattern. Keep the double L in
derivative forms also—FULFILLMENT, INSTILL-
MENT, FULFILLED, etc. Note, however, that in
FULFILL, there is only one L closing the first syllable.

Write the words: ....

                                   ....

                                   ....

21. ANONYMOUS

Remember SYNONYMOUS in chapter 44? The same Greek root, *(nym,* name), is found in ANONYMOUS literally, without a name. The noun is ANONYMITY.

Write the word: ....

Fill in the missing letter or letters, then rewrite the complete word.

1. MASSAC__	....	(RE)
2. MACAB__	....	(RE)
3. MANEUV__	....	(ER)
4. CENT__	....	(ER)
5. MEAG__	....	(ER)
6. AC__	....	(RE)
7. OG__	....	(RE)
8. SAB__	....	(ER)
9. MA__ABRE	....	(C)
10. MA__ACRE	....	(SS)
11. GLAM__R	....	(OU)
12. GLAM__ROUS	....	(O)
13. HON__R	....	(O)
14. NEIGHB__R	....	(O)
15. HUM__R	....	(O)
16. LANG__R	....	(UO)
17. LIQ__R	....	(UO)
18. LINGER__	....	(IE)
19. WE____DAY	....	(DNES)

20. NIN_TEEN .... (E)

21. NIN_TY .... (E)

22. NI_TH .... (N)

23. WIN__Y .... (TR)

24. ILLIT_RATE .... (E)

25. LIT_RATE .... (E)

26. ILLIT_RACY .... (E)

27. LIT_RACY .... (E)

28. LEGIT_MATE .... (I)

29. ILLEGIT_MATE .... (I)

30. LEGIT_MACY .... (I)

31. TEMPER_ENT .... (AM)

32. C__RTESY .... (OU)

33. LICORI__ .... (CE)

34. R__PSODY .... (HA)

35. INSTAL_ .... (L)

36. INSTA__MENT .... (LL)

37. A__ALL .... (PP)

38. FU_FILL .... (L)

39. FULFI__MENT .... (LL)

40. INSTI__MENT .... (LL)

41. INSTI__ .... (LL)

42. DISTI__ .... (LL)

43. FULFI__ED .... (LL)

44. FULFI__ING .... (LL)

45. FU_FILLED   .... (L)

46. MA__ACRED   .... (SS)

47. MAN__VER   .... (EU)

48. LANG__ROUS   .... (UO)

49. I__ITERATE   .... (LL)

50. COURT_OUS   .... (E)

51. COURT_SY   .... (E)

52. ANON_MOUS   .... (Y)

Chapter 48

TEN FINAL PROBLEMS

And now, to wind up what I hope has been a most successful and perhaps eye-opening experience for you with English spelling and all its peculiarities, I ask you to consider a
double handful of pesky problems that puzzle even the most
sophisticated of spellers.

1. S**K**EPTICAL or SC**E**PTICAL?
   Though C is not incorrect following the S, K is far
   preferable in this word and all related forms.
   Write these words:

   S**K**EPTICAL ....

   S**K**EPTIC ....

   S**K**EPTICISM ....

2. PRACTI**C**E or PRACTI**S**E?
   The *noun* must be spelled with a C (not an S), and the
   verb is preferably so spelled, so why make life complicated? Use a C all the time.
   Write these words:

   PRACTI**C**E ....

   to PRACTI**C**E *(v.)* ....

   PRACTI**C**ED *(adj.)* ....

3. PROPHE**C**Y or PROPHE**S**Y? ....

   The *noun* is PROPHE**C**Y (pronounced PROF-e-see),
   the *verb* is PROPHE**S**Y (pronounced PROF-e-sigh).

Consider these sentences:

He made a strange PROPHECY. *(noun)*
What interesting PROPHECIES! *(noun)*
I cannot PROPHESY what will happen. *(verb)*
He PROPHESIED a dark future for his son. (past tense, *verb*)
He PROPHESIES fortune and prosperity. (present tense, *verb*)

There is no such word as *prophecize* or *prophesize*.
Write these words:

PROPHECY *(noun)*   ....

PROPHECIES *(plural noun)*   ....

PROPHESY *(verb)*   ....

PROPHESIED *(verb)*   ....

PROPHESYING *(verb)*   ....

4. FOREWORD or FORWARD?
A FOREWORD is an introduction to a book or other piece of writing—a WORD BEFORE the main part. Do not confuse it with FORWARD, even though it comes up front.
Write these words:

FOREWORD   ....

FORWARD   ....

5. LOATH or LOATHE?
LOATH is an *adjective* meaning reluctant—He is LOATH to go.
     LOATHE is a verb, to hate—I LOATHE him.
Write these words:

LOATH   ....

LOATHE   ....

6. COUNSEL or COUNCIL?
Any reference to *advice* requires the -SEL pattern. You

COUNSEL someone, give him COUNSEL, or act as his COUNSELOR (preferable to *counsellor*). A lawyer is a COUNSELOR, or acts as COUNSEL for the defense. In camp, children are under the guidance of COUNSELORS.

A COUNCIL is a *group* that meets in a legislative or executive capacity. One member of such a group is a COUNCILOR (preferable to *councillor*), or a COUNCILMAN.

Write these words:

COUNSEL   ....

COUNCIL   ....

7. DISK or DISC?
DISK is generally preferable to DISC, unless the word refers to part of the anatomy (a slipped *disc*).
Write the word:

DISK   ....

8. AFFECT
This is the *verb,* used as follows:
    It AFFECTS me strongly.
    How has the weather AFFECTED your plans?
It is also a special noun in psychology meaning *feeling* or *emotional tone*, but is otherwise never a noun in general usage.

Write the word: ....

9. EFFECT
This is the *noun.*
    His voice has a strange EFFECT on me.
    These EFFECTS were unexpected.
And, too, it is a verb with one special meaning only, to *bring about.*
    How can we EFFECT (bring about) our escape?
    Will medical science ever EFFECT (bring about) a cure for cancer?

Write the word: ....

10. WHISKEY or WHISKY?

WHISKEY is the common spelling for American brands—Scotch and Canadian spirits are generally spelled WHISKY. Following the rules we learned recently, the plural of *whiskey* is WHISKEYS, of *whisky*, WHISKIES.

Write these words:

WHISKEY *(domestic)*   ....

WHISKY *(Scotch, Canadian)*   ....

Test Your Learning

Check the correct answer.

1. The preferred spelling is
   (a) skeptical (b) sceptical.   **(a)**
2. The preferred spelling is
   (a) practice, (b) practise.   **(a)**
3. The noun is spelled
   (a) prophesy, (b) prophecy.   **(b)**
4. There is no such word as *prophecize*.
   (a) true, (b) false   **(a)**
5. The past tense of the verb is
   (a) prophecized, (b) prophecied,
   (c) prophesied.   **(c)**
6. The introduction to a book is a
   (a) forward, (b) foreword.   **(b)**
7. A synonym of reluctant is
   (a) loathe, (b) loath.   **(b)**
8. Advice is
   (a) counsel, (b) council.   **(a)**
9. In camp, children have
   (a) councilors, (b) counselors.   **(b)**
10. The preferred spelling, in general use, is
    (a) disc, (b) disk.   **(b)**
11. A bodily part is usually spelled
    (a) disc, (b) disk.   **(a)**

12. As a verb meaning to *influence*, use
    (a) affect, (b) effect. (a)
13. As a verb meaning to *bring about*, use
    (a) affect, (b) effect. (b)
14. As a noun in general use, the word is
    (a) affect, (b) effect. (b)
15. American liquor is spelled
    (a) whisky, (b) whiskey. (b)

Chapter 49

SIXTH REVIEW TEST

I. Check the correct spelling of each word as used in its sentence.

1. (a) It's, (b) Its raining hard.   (a)
2. The dog ate (a) it's, (b) its dinner.   (b)
3. (a) Whose, (b) Who's outside?   (b)
4. (a) Whose, (b) Who's hat did you steal?   (a)
5. They worked (a) their, (b) there hardest.   (a)
6. (a) Their, (b) They're late again.   (b)
7. (a) Their, (b) There are no men in here.   (b)
8. He paid me a great (a) compliment, (b) complement.   (a)
9. The state legislature holds sessions in a building called the (a) capital, (b) capitol.   (b)
10. His (a) fiancé, (b) fiancée ran off with another man.   (b)
11. Did you (a) lose, (b) loose your friend?   (a)
12. The ships were anchored at the (a) navel, (b) naval base.   (b)
13. You're trying (a) two, (b) to, (c) too hard.   (c)
14. (a) Your (b) You're my only friend.   (b)
15. No man can stand the (a) yolk, (b) yoke of slavery.   (b)
16. Is there any point in (a) dying, (b) dyeing this dress?   (b)
17. Do you (a) prophesy, (b) prophicize, (c) prophecy a nuclear war in this century?   (a)
18. The (a) forward, (b) foreword of that book is the only interesting part.   (b)

19. He made a strange (a) prophecy,
    (b) prophesy. (a)
20. I am rather (a) loath, (b) loathe to go. (a)
21. He gave his friend some very good
    (a) council, (b) counsel. (b)
22. He's suffering from a slipped (a) disk,
    (b) disc. (b)
23. The men from Mars arrived in a (a) disc-,
    (b) disk-shaped vehicle. (b)
24. How does his anger (a) affect,
    (b) effect you? (a)
25. What (a) affect, (b) effect does his
    anger have on you? (b)
26. I wish I could (a) affect, (b) effect
    a reconciliation between you two. (b)
27. He bought a quart of Scotch (a) whisky,
    (b) whiskey. (a)

II. Add either -ER or -OR to each word to complete it correctly, then rewrite the complete word.

1. invest- .... (OR)
2. wait- .... (ER)
3. indicat- .... (OR)
4. serv- .... (ER)
5. invent- .... (OR)
6. speak- .... (ER)
7. protect- .... (OR)
8. ancest- .... (OR)
9. retail- .... (ER)
10. prevaricat- .... (OR)
11. elevat- .... (OR)
12. act- .... (OR)

13. distribut-   .... (OR)

14. accelerat-   .... (OR)

15. deposit-   .... (OR)

16. supervis-   .... (OR)

17. view-   .... (ER)

18. speculat-   .... (OR)

19. contribut-   .... (OR)

20. aviat-   .... (OR)

III. Fill in the missing letter or letters, then rewrite.

1. GRAMM_R   .... (A)

2. CALEND_R   .... (A)

3. BEGG_R   .... (A)

4. S_EPTICAL   .... (K)

5. PRACTI_E   .... (C)

6. S_RGEANT   .... (E)

7. L___TENANT   .... (IEU)

8. A__RESS   .... (DD)

9. A_ARTMENT   .... (P)

10. A_KWARD   .... (W)

11. BEN_FIT   .... (E)

12. CHALL_NGE   .... (E)

13. E_CAPE   .... (S)

14. T__SDAY   .... (UE)

15. M_RINGUE   .... (E)

16. COL_ SLAW   .... (E)

17. S____KRAUT .... (AUER)

18. S___RBRATEN .... (AUE)

19. REV__LLE .... (EI)

20. PHI_IPPINES .... (L)

21. FILL_INO .... (P)

22. DO__N'T .... (ES)

23. SOPH_MORE .... (O)

24. HORS D'___VRES .... (OEU)

25. BENEFL_ED .... (T)

26. MAN__VER .... (EU)

27. ATH_ETIC .... (L)

28. DILE__A .... (MM)

29. COMPLE_ION .... (X)

30. CHARAC_ERISTIC .... (T)

31. CE_EBRATE .... (L)

32. SYNON_MOUS .... (Y)

33. UNAN_MOUS .... (I)

34. ANON_MOUS .... (Y)

35. CONNE__ION .... (CT)

IV. Pluralize the following words by adding either S or -ES, then rewrite.

1. TOMATO .... (ES)

2. AUTO .... (S)

3. POTATO .... (ES)

4. CELLO .... (S)

5. HERO .... (ES)

6. PIANO .... (S)

7. ECHO .... (ES)

8. EMBRYO .... (S)

9. MOSQUITO .... (ES)

10. ZERO .... (S)

11. MOTTO .... (ES)

12. BANJO .... (S)

13. VETO .... (ES)

14. HOBO .... (S)

15. NO .... (ES)

16. SOLO .... (S)

17. TORPEDO .... (ES)

18. STUDIO .... (S)

19. NEGRO .... (ES)

20. ESKIMO .... (S)

21. EMBARGO .... (ES)

22. RADIO .... (S)

23. INNUENDO .... (ES)

24. MULATTO .... (ES)

25. MANIFESTO .... (ES)

V. Each word below is deliberately misspelled. Cross it out and rewrite it correctly.

1. couragous

....   (COURAGEOUS)

2. religous

.... (RELIGIOUS)

3. irrelidgious

.... (IRRELIGIOUS)

4. sacreligous

.... (SACRILEGIOUS)

5. pidgeon

.... (PIGEON)

6. dungon

.... (DUNGEON)

7. blugeon

.... (BLUDGEON)

8. monastary

.... (MONASTERY)

9. millinary

.... (MILLINERY)

10. dysentary

.... (DYSENTERY)

11. cemetary

.... (CEMETERY)

12. elementery

.... (ELEMENTARY)

13. secretery

.... (SECRETARY)

14. dictionery

....   (DICTIONARY)

15. adversery

....   (ADVERSARY)

16. temporery

....   (TEMPORARY)

17. massacer

....   (MASSACRE)

18. glamor

....   (GLAMOUR)

19. glamourous

....   (GLAMOROUS)

20. langour

....   (LANGUOR)

21. lingeray

....   (LINGERIE)

22. Wensday

....   (WEDNESDAY)

23. nineth

....   (NINTH)

24. ninteen

....   (NINETEEN)

25. ninty

....   (NINETY)

26. wintery

.... (WINTRY)

27. illitterate

.... (ILLITERATE)

28. legitamate

.... (LEGITIMATE)

29. temperment

.... (TEMPERAMENT)

30. courtisy

.... (COURTESY)

31. inteligible

.... (INTELLIGIBLE)

32. elegible

.... (ELIGIBLE)

33. ilegible

.... (ILLEGIBLE)

34. licorish

.... (LICORICE)

35. rapsody

.... (RHAPSODY)

36. instalment

.... (INSTALLMENT)

37. apalled

.... (APPALLED)

38. fullfil

.... (FULFILL)

39. instil

.... (INSTILL)

40. distil

.... (DISTILL)

41. skilful

.... (SKILLFUL)

42. wilful

.... (WILLFUL)

Chapter **50.**
YOUR MASTER SPELLING TEST

English spelling should no longer be a mystery to you. It should no longer be frustrating, confusing, or painful. For —if you have worked successfully on the 49 preceding chapters—you have met the enemy and conquered him.

Slowly, methodically, with practice and calculated repetition, you have trained your mind, your eyes, and your fingers on the 1,100 most commonly misspelled words in the language.

You know, now—and not only intellectually but in a sense also physically—when to write -ISE, when -IZE, when -YZE; when to end a word with -ARY or -ERY; when to use -IE and -EI; when to double a final consonant and when to leave it alone; when to keep the E before -ABLE and when to discard it; when to insert a K after final C, and when not to; when to use -ABLE, and when to use -IBLE; and many, many more things that only careful training and repeated practice can teach you.

You are now able, as a result, to write a letter, or a report, or a memo, or an article, or even a whole book without committing any errors in spelling. What's more, you're *sure* of your ability, you feel secure and self-confident that any word you're likely to use you can, without a moment's hesitation, spell correctly.

So, just as a finishing touch, and more for its psychological value than for any teaching purposes, I ask you to test yourself on 100 of the words we've covered—the 100 demons most frequently misspelled by the average, untrained person. You will, of course, without any effort or trouble, make a perfect score, and you will then have official proof of how close to expert you now are.

Do the test lightly in pencil, check your answers, then

erase what you've written and offer the same test to anyone you consider really literate. *And please conceal that smug smile when you go over the results with him.*

An Acid Test of Spelling Ability

I. Each of the following 50 words is offered in its correct form and in one or more popular misspellings. Check the pattern you trust.

1. (a) drunkeness, (b) drunkenness.
2. (a) coolly, (b) cooly.
3. (a) incidently, (b) incidentally.
4. (a) embarrassment, (b) embarassment,
   (c) embarrassement.
5. (a) sieze, (b) seize.
6. (a) allotted, (b) alotted, (c) alloted.
7. (a) alright, (b) allright, (c) all right.
8. (a) occurance, (b) occurrance, (c) occurrence.
9. (a) chagrined, (b) chagrinned.
10. (a) inoculate, (b) innoculate, (c) inocculate.
11. (a) reccomend, (b) recommend.
12. (a) occassional, (b) occasional.
13. (a) annoint, (b) anoint.
14. (a) exhilarated, (b) exhillarated, (c) exhilerated.
15. (a) iridescent, (b) irredescent, (c) irridescent.
16. (a) dissipate, (b) disippate, (c) dissapate.
17. (a) friccasee, (b) fricassee.
18. (a) battalion, (b) batallion.
19. (a) seive, (b) sieve.
20. (a) persistant, (b) persistent.
21. (a) insistant, (b) insistent.
22. (a) predictible, (b) predictable.
23. (a) superintendant, (b) superintendent.
24. (a) perseverance, (b) perserverance, (c) perseverence.
25. (a) inadvertant, (b) inadvertent.
26. (a) desparate, (b) desperate.
27. (a) separate, (b) seperate.
28. (a) catagory, (b) category.
29. (a) mathamatics, (b) mathematics.

30. (a) lonliness, (b) loneliness.
31. (a) argument, (b) arguement.
32. (a) irresistible, (b) irrisistable, (c) irrisistible.
33. (a) indispensible, (b) indespensable, (c) indispensable.
34. (a) sacrilegious, (b) sacreligious.
35. (a) disappoint, (b) dissapoint.
36. (a) hairbrained, (b) harebrained.
37. (a) nickle, (b) nickel.
38. (a) paraffin, (b) parrafin.
39. (a) geneology, (b) genealogy.
40. (a) repitition, (b) repetition.
41. (a) license, (b) liscence, (c) lisence.
42. (a) desiccate, (b) dessicate.
43. (a) quizzes, (b) quizes.
44. (a) recconoiter, (b) reconnoiter.
45. (a) apochryphal, (b) apocryphal.
46. (a) esophagus, (b) esophagous.
47. (a) asisstant, (b) assistant.
48. (a) surprise, (b) supprise, (c) surprize.
49. (a) benifited, (b) benefitted, (c) benefited.
50. (a) heros, (b) heroes.

II. Of the following 50 words, exactly half are spelled correctly; the other half are misspelled. Check the space if you consider the form correct; if not, rewrite the word in the pattern that appeals to you.

1. kidnaped ....

2. descendant ....

3. descriminate ....

4. persuit ....

5. dumfound ....

6. gaiety ....

7. developement ....

8. beseige ....

9. weird ....

10. inimitible ....

11. canceled ....

12. dispair ....

13. millionnaire ....

14. titillate ....

15. neice ....

16. scintilate ....

17. truely ....

18. disheveled ....

19. dictionery ....

20. woolly ....

21. guttural ....

22. definately ....

23. numskull ....

24. yoeman ....

25. protruberant ....

26. vicious ....

27. sourkraut ....

28. obbligato ....

29. macabre ....

30. cattarrh ....

31. ecstacy ....

32. millennium ....

33. imacculate ....

34. plebeian ....

35. acommodate ....

36. bettor ....

37. paralyze ....

38. stupefy ....

39. Phillipines ....

40. threshhold ....

41. drier ....

42. minerology ....

43. defense ....

44. fulfill ....

45. curvaceous ....

46. hypocrasy ....

47. skillful ....

48. violoncello ....

49. dilletante ....

50. supersede ....

KEY TO I

1-b	11-b	21-b	31-a	41-a
2-a	12-b	22-b	32-a	42-a
3-b	13-b	23-b	33-c	43-a
4-b	14-a	24-a	34-a	44-b
5-b	15-a	25-b	35-a	45-b
6-a	16-a	26-b	36-b	46-a
7-c	17-b	27-a	37-b	47-b
8-c	18-a	28-b	38-a	48-a
9-a	19-b	29-b	39-b	49-c
10-a	20-b	30-b	40-b	50-b

KEY TO II

1-√
2-√
3-discriminate
4-pursuit
5-√
6-√
7-development
8-besiege
9-√
10-inimitable
11-√
12-despair
13-millionaire
14-√
15-niece
16-scintillate
17-truly
18-√
19-dictionary
20-√
21-√
22-definitely
23-√
24-yeoman
25-protuberant

26-√
27-sauerkraut
28-√
29-√
30-catarrh
31-ecstasy
32-√
33-immaculate
34-√
35-accommodate
36-√ (one who bets)
37-√
38-√
39-Philippines
40-threshold
41-√
42-mineralogy
43-√
44. fullfill
45-√
46-hypocrisy
47-√
48-√
49-dilettante
50-√

Scoring

In Part I, allow 1% for each correct choice.

In Part II, take 1% if you checked a correct spelling or if you were able to rewrite in its *proper* form any word spelled incorrectly.

The average educated person who is not a trained speller will likely do no better than 50%. Anyone who has studied this book conscientiously and thoroughly should make a perfect or near-perfect score.

INDEX

(Numbers refer to chapters, NOT pages.)

assassin, 14
assassination, 14
assess, 14
assessment, 14
assist, 39
assistant, 39
athlete, 44
athletic, 44
attendance, 17
attendant, 17
attorneys, 45
audible, 26
aviator, 43
awful, 22
awkward, 44

B

bachelor, 43
baited—bated, 30
balloon, 9
banqueter, 11
barely, 22
bated—baited, 30
battalion, 14
bearable, 28
beautiful, 45
beautifying, 45
befriend, 7
beggar, 11, 44
beginner, 43
believable, 21
believe, 4, 5
benefit, 44
beneficial, 44
besiege, 4, 5
betrayed, 45
bettor, 43
biasing, 11
bidding, 11
bivouacked, 35
blamable, 21, 24
bludgeon, 46
bony, 21

bookkeeper, 3
boys, 45
breakable, 24
brief, 4
broccoli, 36
buccaneer, 36
buggy, 11
business, 31
busying, 45
butcher, 43

C

caffeine, 5
cagey, 22
calendar, 44
canceled, 10
canceling, 11
cannon—canon, 30
canon—cannon, 30
canvas—canvass, 30
canvass—canvas, 30
capable, 25
capital—capitol, 42
capitol—capital, 42
caress, 13
catarrh, 39
category, 19
ceiling, 4
celebrate, 44
cemetery, 46
chagrined, 11, 39
chagrining, 39
challenge, 44
changeable, 20, 21
characteristic, 44
chastise, 2, 40
chastising, 2
chief, 5
chord—cord, 30
chow mein, 6
chrysanthemum, 39
cinnamon, 36
circumcise, 40

classifiable, 28
classify, 34
codeine, 5
coercible, 28
coincidentally, 3
cole slaw, 44
colicky, 35
collaborate, 9
collapsible, 27, 28
collectible, 27
colossal, 14
combustible, 26
coming, 21
commendable, 25
commentary, 46
commentator, 43
commitment, 11
committed, 10
committee, 36
communicable, 28
comparable, 24
comparative, 19
comparison, 19
compatible, 26
compelled, 10
competition, 31
complement—compli-
    ment, 42
complexion, 44
compliment—comple-
    ment, 42
comprehensible, 26, 33
comprise, 40
compromise, 40
concede, 34
conceit, 4
conceited, 4
conceive, 4
conceived, 4
concurred, 10
concurrence, 11, 16
concurrent, 11, 16
confectionery, 46
conference, 11

conferred, 10
confidence, 16
confident, 16
confusion, 21
connoisseur, 37
conqueror, 43
conscience, 7, 33
conscious, 33
consensus, 44
conspirator, 43
contagion, 46
contagious, 46
contemptible, 27, 28
contractible, 27
contributor, 43
controlled, 10
convalescent, 33
convertible, 27
convincible, 26
coolly, 3
copyright, 39
cord—chord, 30
correctable, 24, 27
corroborate, 37
corrodible, 27
corruptible, 28
council, 48
counsel, 48
counseled, 10
counterfeit, 6
courageous, 46
courtesy, 47
coyly, 45
coyness, 45
credible, 26
cried, 45
crier, 45
cries, 45
culpable, 25
curvaceous, 39

D

debatable, 21

deceit, 4
deceitful, 4
deceive, 4
deceiver, 4
deceiving, 4
decisiveness, 22
defense, 33
defensible, 26
deference, 11
deferment, 11
deficient, 4, 7
definitely, 19
deign, 6
delectable, 25
demagogue, 19
demonstrable, 25
dependable, 24
dependence, 16
dependent, 16
deplorable, 21, 24
depositor, 43
descendant, 17
describable, 21
describe, 19
description, 19
desert—dessert, 30
desiccated, 13
desirable, 21, 24
desiring, 21
desirous, 21
despair, 19
desperate, 19
despicable, 24
despise, 2, 40
despising, 2
dessert—desert, 30
destroys, 45
detectable, 27
deterred, 10
deterrence, 11, 16
deterrent, 11, 16
development, 3, 22
devise, 2, 19, 40
devising, 2

diaries, 45
diarrhea, 39
dictionary, 46
die—dye, 42
difference, 16
different, 16
diffidence, 16
diffident, 16
digestible, 28
dilemma, 44
dilettante, 14
disadvantageous, 46
disagree, 29, 38
disagreeable, 28, 38
disagreement, 38
disappear, 3
disapprove, 3
disappoint, 3
disc, 48
discernible, 27, 28
discriminate, 19
disguise, 40
disheveled, 31
disk, 48
dismissible, 26
dispelling, 11
dispensable, 24, 26
dissatisfy, 3
dissimilar, 3
dissipate, 14
dissipation, 14
distill, 47
distributor, 43
divide, 19
divisible, 26
doesn't, 44
donkeys, 45
drier, 45
dries, 45
drunkenness, 3
drying, 45
dryly, 45
dryness, 45
duly, 22

NOTES